Lexington
MINUTE MAN SIX

Five-passenger Touring Car, with two auxiliary seats, $1755 f. o. b. factory

—for Substantial People Who Appreciate Values

OUT into the spring sunshine the Lexington carries the family, wherever the road leads and wherever its owner desires to go, with complete satisfaction all the way.

As time goes on, the first favorable impression ripens into warm admiration for Lexington construction and mechanical perfection.

Ingenuity is expressed in every part of this sturdy car. From its frame more than a hundred separate parts have been eliminated. The result has decreased its weight and added materially to its strength and long-life.

The Lexington one-finger emergency brake, operated with the pressure of a finger, checks its speed with an action at once gentle yet positive.

Fuel economy is accomplished by the Moore Multiple Exhaust System, *exclusively* Lexington, which gives more horsepower per piston displacement.

Its design is strikingly new without the slightest tendency toward freakishness.

Its accommodations, roomy comfort and conveniences become immediately apparent.

When you take the wheel, and feel its powerful motor lift you out of the congested traffic and over the steep grade; —when you know that your Lexington is conserving your gasoline, giving its maximum power while continually guarding against needless waste; then you experience the satisfaction which comes *only* with Lexington ownership.

All of these superiorities are made possible by Lexington management, manufacture and skill.

Other *strictly* Lexington features are oilless bushings, non-metallic universal joints, lightweight yet powerful construction.

Ten plants, specializing in motor car parts, are affiliated with and contribute to Lexington success.

Lexington dealers can give you immediate deliveries.

See your nearest Lexington dealer today, or write us.

Lexington Motor Company Connersville, Ind., U. S. A.

EAST

Fearon's
OUR CENTURY 1910-1920   1tr

AMERICAN HISTORY

DATE DUE

A Note from the Editor

You are about to take a journey backward in time. Your means of transportation will be the written word and some glorious photographs. Your journey will take you, decade by decade, through the 20th century . . . our century.

Many of the events described in each issue of *Our Century* magazine are famous. Some have perhaps been forgotten. Many of the people were extraordinary, some merely ordinary, a few certainly evil. But all these events and people have one thing in common: they have made this century a fascinating and momentous one.

All of us who worked on *Our Century* hope you find your journey into the past interesting and educational. And most of all we hope you enjoy these "snapshots in time" as much as we enjoyed recapturing them for you.

Tony Napolo
Editor-in-Chief, *Our Century*

Statistics

	1910	1920
Population of the United States	91.9 million	105.7 million
Number of states in the United States	46	48
Number of cities with populations over 1 million	3	3
Population by race:		
White	81.7 million	94.8 million
Negro	9.8 million	10.4 million
American Indian	265,683	242,959
Asian	143,688	172,211
Other	3,175	11,404
Population by sex:		
Male	47.3 million	53.9 million
Female	44.6 million	51.8 million
Population per square mile	30.9	35.5
Number of persons 100 years old and over	3,555	4,267
Three leading causes of death in the U.S.	Heart disease Tuberculosis Bright's disease	Heart disease Tuberculosis Bright's disease
Largest city in the world	London	London
Number of national parks	20	29
Unemployment rate	5.9%	4.0%
Average hourly wage for carpenters	63¢	$1.14
Average monthly salary for teachers	$62.23	$78.10
Number of working children by sex:	(aged 10–13)	(aged 10–15)
Boys	609,030	714,248
Girls	286,946	346,610
Number of candymakers	30,943	*
People working as servants	*	1.2 million
Number of actors in the U.S.	28,297	28,361
Illiteracy rate	7.7%	6%
Number of students in schools and colleges	21.1 million	21.7 million
Prices:		
postage stamp	5¢	5¢
pound of coffee	5¢	47¢
pack of Camels	*	18¢
Studebaker Electric automobile	$1,750	*
Oldsmobile Eight	*	$1,895
girl's bloomer dress	$1.50 to $3.00	*
boy's knickerbocker suit	*	$12.50

* Figures not available

Fearon's OUR CENTURY

Our Century is a trademark of David S. Lake Publishers. *Our Century 1910-1920.* Copyright © 1989 by David S. Lake Publishers, 500 Harbor Boulevard, Belmont, California 94002. All rights reserved. No part of this publication may be reproduced by any means, transmitted, or translated into a machine language without written permission from the publisher.

ISBN 0–8224–5077–1

1. 9 8 7 6 5 4 3 2 1
Writer: Karen Liberatore
Designer: Detta Penna

All photographs: The Bettmann Archive, with the following exceptions: pp. 4, 7, 9: Library of Congress; pp. 5, 6, 23, 48, 64: National Archives; pp. 24 (top left), 55, 57 (bottom right): UPI/Bettmann Newsphotos. Advertisements on end papers: The D'Arcy Collection, University of Illinois at Urbana-Champaign.

1910–1920

Employment
Workers Heading North

The farm laborers pictured below are shown working in the apple orchards of West Virginia in 1910. By the time the decade came to a close they were a dying breed. These were the years that Americans headed north. Thousands of workers were lured away from the rural, agricultural areas of the South. All were headed for jobs in the larger industrial cities: New York, Philadelphia, Chicago, and San Francisco.

In 1910, agriculture was the main occupation among Americans. More than 12.6 million people worked on farms and dairies, either as owners or hired help. In that same year, 10.6 million workers held jobs in manufacturing and mechanical trades. That number included those working in the new business, automobile manufacturing.

By 1920, these numbers had flip-flopped. The manufacturing/mechanical field had 12.8 million workers, and agriculture had 10.9 million.

As for wages, a farm worker made an average $2.52 a day (without room and board) in 1910. In

1920, that figure had risen to $3.68. In comparison, a big city carpenter or plumber in 1920 made $1.25 an hour. Based on a 44-hour work week, the daily pay came to about $11.00. Labor unions explained the difference. There were no unions for farm workers. But in the cities, unions helped workers secure better pay, job safety, and benefits.

There was another important factor that sent workers from the rural areas to the North. As the decade progressed, there were fewer jobs available on the farms. This job shortage had to do with the effects of the Great War. Food was a valuable commodity in Europe. Farmlands there had been ruined by four years of fighting. As a result, American farmers could make more money by raising fewer crops. And profits could be further increased by cutting back on the number of laborers.

For example, 107 million acres of corn—America's number one crop—were valued at $1.5 million in 1912. In 1919, 97 million acres of corn were worth $3.7 million. That was nearly a 150 percent *increase* in value and a 10 percent *decrease* in the number of acres cultivated.

A report filed in 1918 pointed out another significant fact. It showed that for the first time in America's history, the center of the Negro population had shifted northward. Negroes had always been the traditional farm workers. Their move to the cities signaled that the change in the way America worked was not a fluke. It seemed to be a definite trend.

Child Labor

Many of America's workers are not adults. As the photograph above illustrates, young children supply labor in a number of industries. Despite periods of unemployment, industry is growing fast. Employers look for cheap labor—and children provide it.

During the decade, the greatest number of child workers, 647,309, worked on farms and dairies. But large numbers of children were ⇨

Employers look for cheap labor— children provide it.

working in factories and mines as well. As the decade ended, 185,337 children under the age of 15 were working in the manufacturing trades. Of that number, 54,649 worked in textile mills, such as the 12-year-old girl pictured here. More than 54,000 were employed as maids and servants. And another 7,191 children, like the Pennsylvania boys pictured on the previous page, worked in the mines.

Public outcries against child labor grew as the decade ended. Among those who championed laws to protect children was Lewis Hine, the photographer whose pictures are shown on pages 5 and 6. In 1918, a law was passed that fined employers who worked children for more than eight hours a day. But reform has not come quickly. Many people charge that American industry could benefit more in the long run if children were better educated. ■

Public outcries against child labor grew as the decade ended.

Trains and Ships Still Transporting Most Goods

Trains and ships, including the Mississippi River boats pictured above, remained America's primary means of transporting its goods around the country. But throughout the period, the automobile was beginning to play a role of greater importance.

More and more workers were moving north. They went to Michigan where Ford, Chevrolet, and other automobile factories were located. Of the 22 fastest growing cities in America, five were in Michigan. The two fastest growing cities were Hamtramck and Highland Park. In Hamtramck, the increase in population between 1910 and 1920 was a whopping 1,266 percent. In Highland Park, it was 1,028 percent.

"The famed highways of the ancient Romans will pale by comparison."

By 1920, the automobile was seen as the savior of agriculture. That year, the high prices farmers had enjoyed during and shortly after the war took a nose dive. In 1919, a bushel of corn was worth $1.34. A year later, the price had dropped almost in half, to 67 cents.

Many in government warned that rural areas were facing financial ruin. Some called for a "general policy of transportation."

They wanted construction of more roads linked with interstate highways. They saw this as one way to improve transportation between rural areas and cities. Rural areas could then become self-sufficient. Goods manufactured or grown there could be motored out for less money than by railroad.

By 1920, plans were being made to greatly increase the number of U.S. highways and roads. Never in America's history had the federal government made an organized effort to connect roads with highways. Before, roads were constructed when needed, with no thought to a national system. "The famed highways of the ancient Romans will pale by comparison," one writer said of the plan. ∎

Education

More Schools, More Courses, More Students

Economic growth in the United States was the major influence on education in the decade 1910–1920. Educators recognized that there was only one way to keep improving industrial output. And that way was to teach young people more than the basics of reading, writing and arithmetic.

On the high-school level, many new courses were added to the curriculum. These courses included vocational training, agricultural science, home economics, general science, health, music, and art.

On the elementary school level, educational reform focused on preschoolers. In 1918, five states set up the nation's first public kindergartens. Their decision was influenced by the lobbying efforts of women's organizations. The Congress of Mothers, for example, was in favor of kindergartens. They said that kindergartens "prepare children not only for schoolwork, but also for vital social interaction."

As the decade opened, there were 21.1 million young people in American schools, elementary through college. That figure was nearly one-fifth of the total population of the United States. (The figure includes students enrolled in business and agricultural schools, reform schools, schools for the deaf and the blind, Indian schools, Negro schools and orphan schools.) Of the total, 18.5 million children were enrolled in elementary schools. Another 1.3 million went to high school. And 200,150 were studying in colleges, universities, and the higher-education vocational schools.

In 1911, there were 11,277 public high schools; 2,168 private high schools; and 596 colleges. Of the college population, male students were the majority. There were 120,380 men enrolled versus 60,767 women.

Agriculture Still First

By the end of the decade, the number of public high schools had increased to nearly 14,000. In addition, nearly 100 new colleges had opened. And there were approximately 600,000 new students in schools, raising the total to 21.7 million nationwide.

In 1919, the most notable change in the student population was seen at the college and university level. Because of the Great War, the number of male students enrolled had dropped to 97,399. In the same year there were 79,941 females attending colleges.

Agriculture remained the number one trade among students bound for higher education. Among the professional degrees sought, law students led the way with 20,842. Next came medicine with 14,800; dentistry 8,513; theology 7,105; and veterinary medicine, 956. ∎

Five states set up the nation's first kindergartens.

"Separate But Equal"

The students pictured below are studying history at the Tuskegee Institute. This high school in Alabama was founded in 1881 by Booker T. Washington, the famed Negro educator. The Institute is a privately funded school with an emphasis on vocational training. It is considered one of the best schools in the nation for Negroes whose children normally attend segregated public schools.

Many Americans believe that "separate but equal" segregated schools have hurt the Negro population. According to census figures in 1910, the illiteracy rate among rural Negroes was 36.1 compared to a rural white rate of 5.8. Among those Americans working to change this imbalance in education is Julius Rosenwald of Chicago. Rosenwald has donated more than $1 million toward the construction of 1,633 schoolhouses in 14 southern states. ∎

Fashion

Hemlines Going Up

"**S**hocking" is the word some people use to describe the decade's trend in women's fashions. As the photograph below shows, shorter skirts were the big news.

By 1920, newspapers reported that hemlines were "astonishingly nearer" the knee than ever before. Experts predict that the trend will continue. They say that "short" will be the watchword for the next several years.

Shorter skirts make quite a contrast to the "hobble skirts" shown in the 1910 photograph (below right). These high-fashion gowns were often "tied" near the hem by a straight band. Paris designers created the style, which caught on quickly in America.

For years the hobble skirt has been a favorite fashion. Women have worn them even while complaining that "hobbles" were uncomfortable and hard to walk in. When the hobble was first introduced, it was praised for its elegant cut and careful attention to design. Some hobble gowns—designed to be as straight as a stalk—were likened to mushrooms. The women who wore them often added to the look by wearing wide-brimmed hats. The hat was supposed to look like the cap of a mushroom.

The Great War has been an influence on women's fashions. Many women entered the work force to replace men who had gone to war. Their needs were for practical clothing. Hobble skirts, obviously, just wouldn't do. They looked for clothing that was free and easy.

In reality, the styles adopted during and after the war were products of the war itself. Most of the fashion houses in Paris were shut down during the war. Those that took their place brought modern methods. They used new, synthetic fibers and improved production equipment. By the end of the decade, more clothes than ever were available. They looked good, too. Newly created dyes gave clothes a never-before-seen brightness.

Some designers warn that the changes in this decade signal the end of an era. They say the era of "femininity, variety, and refinement" has come to an end. In its place, they see dull, mass-produced "uniformity." ∎

A Floating Palace

The "Unsinkable" *Titanic* Sails on Maiden Voyage

The world had never seen anything quite like the steamship *Titanic*. It was a "floating palace" of fine furniture and artworks, stained-glass windows and elegant woodworking. It offered passengers unheard of luxuries on the high seas: a saltwater swimming pool, a complete gymnasium, and electric heaters in all the staterooms.

The builders of the *Titanic* saw their ship as a sea-going hotel of the highest class. Its most impressive room was the one passengers saw first. The main entrance hall had a sweeping grand staircase that led to the decks above.

But in the spring of 1912 the *Titanic* was best known as a scientific wonder. The ship was the largest and fastest vessel ever built. Experts said it was the "last word" in modern construction. The ship combined a "unique" system of propellers with structural strength. The *Titanic* had eight decks. It was 882½ feet long—"twice as long as the Great Pyramid in Egypt is tall," wrote one admirer. The *Titanic* cost $10 million, and took three years to build. The ship's owners, White Star Lines, boasted of its power and size. In fact, they proudly proclaimed their *Titanic* "unsinkable."

On April 10, 1912, a total of 2,340 passengers and crew boarded the *Titanic* in Southampton, England. The "weather was fine and the sea calm." The excited passengers and crew eagerly awaited the ship's maiden voyage across the Atlantic Ocean. Among those headed for New York City on this history-making trip were families, students and immigrants. One of the passengers was J.

Bruce Ismay. It was Ismay who first conceived the idea of building the *Titanic*. Now he was president of the company that owned the steamship line.

Also on board were Colonel John J. Astor and his young bride, Madeline. Astor was one of the wealthiest and most famous men in America. In fact, many of the passengers on board for the first trip were rich. Newspapers reported that the total worth of the passengers was $495 million. Added to that, the fancy new ship carried a $5 million cargo of diamonds, and Mrs. Astor herself brought with her $6 million in jewels.

After four days at sea, the *Titanic* had completed nearly two-thirds of its journey. On the night of April 14 it was approximately 1,000 miles from New York. And the huge, modern luxury liner was "speeding for a maiden-voyage record," as one passenger later recalled. He also remembered how clear the moonless night sky was, how "glassy" the ocean looked, and how cold it was outside. "In fact after dinner it was almost too cold to be out on deck at all," he said.

The chill came with the territory. At this point in the journey the *Titanic* had reached the iceberg fields off the tip of Newfoundland. And this year the fields were particularly dangerous. Vessels had reported being shut in by ice stretching to the horizon in all directions.

The *Titanic* hit the iceberg fields going full throttle. Critics later charged that the ship was traveling too fast in its bid to break the speed record.

In the end, though, nothing could have saved the *Titanic*. It never saw what it hit. ∎

Disaster at Sea

Iceberg Rips *Titanic's* Side Like a Giant Can Opener

> "Goodbye boys," the captain told his crew. "I'm going to follow the ship."

At 11:40 p.m. on April 14, 1912, the *Titanic* hit the submerged portion of a giant iceberg. At 2:20 A.M., the "unsinkable" *Titanic* sunk.

Survivors described the deadly impact as feeling like nothing more than a "jolt." And they said people joked about it then. But that jolt hit the *Titanic* where it was most vulnerable—in its side. The iceberg opened up the ship like a can opener, letting the icy sea water gush in through the 300-foot gash it left. When the end came, two and one-half hours later, the *Titanic* stood upright in the sea "looming black against the sky." Then it plunged downward, head first into the water.

"With a quiet, slanting dive, the ship disappeared," one surviving passenger remembered. And the worst was yet to come. To the horror of those on board, the *Titanic* was not carrying enough lifeboats for all its passengers.

"There fell on the ear the most appalling noise that human beings ever listened to," the survivor recalled later. The horrible sounds were the cries of fellow passengers struggling in the icy cold water, crying for help.

"I think those sounds will be one of the things the rescued will find difficult to erase from memory," the survivor said. "We are all trying hard not to think of it."

Survivors also remember how calm everyone was at first, even as the ship tilted deeper into the sea. No one expected the great *Titanic* to actually sink. Even as passengers were loaded onto lifeboats, panic played a small part in farewells. Colonel Astor's wife recalled later

The sinking of the *Titanic* was the worst accident in the history of ocean-going vessels. It was completing its maiden voyage from England to New York City when the submerged portion of an iceberg ripped it apart, killing 1,503 of its more than 2,200 passengers.

that he simply said to her, "Goodbye, dear, I'll join you shortly."

Of the more that 2,200 passengers aboard the *Titanic*, 745 survived, most of them women and children. The dead, numbering 1,503, included the captain, E. J. Smith. He refused to be rescued. "Goodbye boys," he declared to his crew. "I'm going to follow the ship."

Among the victims were many of the rich and famous, including Colonel Astor, journalists, and a respected military aide to President William Howard Taft. Most of the dead were men. "Women and children to the lifeboats first" was the rule enforced by the *Titanic's* crew. Only later was it discovered that the lifeboats on board had room for only half the passengers.

Among those men who did survive was J. Bruce Ismay, the *Titanic's* creator. He reportedly was among the first passengers to be loaded onto a lifeboat.

At dawn on April 15, after four hours of drifting in the frigid dark waters, the lifeboats were finally spotted. The survivors, many of them wearing only their night clothes, were

taken aboard the steamer, *Carpathia*. It had been 58 miles away when the *Titanic* had sent its first S.O.S. through the wireless. "Sinking by the head. Have cleared boats and filled them with women and children." That was the last message the *Titanic* sent to the world.

Three days later, on Thursday, April 18, the *Carpathia* steamed into New York City. It was greeted solemnly by relatives of the *Titanic's* passengers and a curious crowd stretching two blocks deep.

"The tragedy of the *Titanic* was written on the faces of nearly all her survivors," a reporter later wrote. It was then that the world heard of the "heroes" of the *Titanic's* sinking. That's how survivors described the doomed members of the *Titanic's* band, who kept on playing as they went down with the ship.

"One of the things that lingers gratefully in the minds of the survivors was the music that floated to them over the waters," the reporter wrote. "To the straining ears of the people in the boats came first 'When We Meet Beyond.' And later, when the great ship had sagged still deeper in the

water, the band played softly, 'Nearer My God to Thee.'" ■

Maiden Voyage Ends in Tragedy

The loss of the *Titanic* was the worst maritime disaster ever recorded. The nearest approach to such an unfortunate fate, a newspaper reported, was the cruise of the *Naronic*. Twenty years before the *Titanic* went down, the *Naronic*, carrying about 300 passengers, steamed out of New York and was never heard from again. The ship was owned by White Star Lines, the same company that owned the *Titanic*.

In the last 50 years icebergs have been responsible for 12 disasters at sea. The last occurred in 1903, when 22 lives were lost. The worst, until now, occurred in 1864, when an immigrant ship was lost close to where the *Titanic* went down. More than 150 persons drowned in that disaster.

The Murder That Triggered a World War

In the summer of 1914, the Archduke Francis Ferdinand was the heir to the throne of Austria-Hungary. On June 28, the archduke and his wife visited Sarajevo, the capital of Bosnia. Bosnia was a Balkan province controlled by Austria-Hungary. Serbia, Bosnia's neighbor, was a rival of Austria-Hungary. The Serbian people believed strongly that they had a natural right to control both

---

"It's now or never. We must finish the Serbs off for good."

Bosnia and another neighboring province. Many people in Bosnia, including groups of Bosnian revolutionaries, felt stronger ties to Serbia than to Austria-Hungary.

As Ferdinand and his wife rode through the streets of Sarajevo, a bomb was thrown into their car. They barely escaped death. "The bomb did not reach its target, thanks to the quick reaction of the archduke," an eyewitness said. "He picked it up from the car seat and threw it into the street. I could not believe my eyes."

Eight people, however, were injured when the bomb exploded.

That afternoon, as the royal couple returned from visiting the bomb's victims, a second assassin succeeded where the first had failed.

Gavrilo Princip, a 19-year-old student, fired seven shots at the couple as their car passed. The archduke was killed instantly. His wife died en route to the hospital. The assassin was a member of a Serbian terrorist group. He told the police he wanted to "avenge the Serbs for the oppression they had been suffering."

There was no direct evidence then that the assassin was connected to the Serbian government. But even at that, Austria-Hungary and Germany reacted to the deaths by accusing the Serbian government of murder.

"It is now or never. We must finish the Serbs off for good," wrote Germany's emperor, Kaiser Wilhelm II.

The Sides Are Drawn

War arrived in stages after the assassination of the archduke. A month after his death, Austria-Hungary declared war on Serbia. Two days later, Russia, Serbia's ally, mobilized its army.

On August 1, 1914, Germany and Russia went to war. As Russia's ally, France, too, became Germany's enemy. On August 2, before war against France had been formally declared, the German army marched into Belgium. Its goal was Paris. With Germany's invasion of Belgium, Great Britain was the next to enter the war, siding with its allies, Russia and France.

Eventually the rest of Europe, and finally the United States, went to war as well. Although it became known as the Great War, in truth, it was the worst nightmare of horrors and devastation the world had ever seen. ∎

The End of Peace in Europe

Balance of Power Topples

To most of the world, Europe seemed a safe, secure place in the spring of 1914. And for good reason. There hadn't been a major military conflict in Europe in 100 years.

But ongoing peace was not to be. For decades the countries of Europe—France and Germany particularly—had been building up their armies and their supply of weapons. Along with the military buildup, alliances had been formed between several governments. These "friendships" were often based on ties among royal families. In effect, they separated Europe into two armed camps. One was the German Empire. The other included Russia and the rest of Europe. (See the chart below this story.)

The countries' leaders said that these alliances formed a "balance of power." But this "balance" was shaky. Government leaders weren't content with the empires they already controlled. They wanted more territory.

So, they kept expanding. They used economic and political pressures to take over weaker countries. This policy of all-out expansion came to be called imperialism. By the beginning of the 20th century, imperialism was spreading all over the world.

In 1914, two of the major imperialist nations clashed. Russia and Germany had their eyes on the same area of Europe. That area was called the Balkan States. The Balkans were in south central Europe along the Adriatic Sea. That location was important for Russia and Germany. The area provided access to the Mediterranean Sea for the Russians. And the Germans needed it to pass to the Near and Far East.

In many countries, the people themselves fueled their leaders' imperialism. Ordinary citizens became patriotic to the extreme. They believed that their countries could do no wrong. That mood blossomed in a frenzy of pride called nationalism. And it was nationalism that lit the fires of war. In Serbia, ultrapatriotism crossed the line into terrorism. There, die-hard Serbians did not support their government's allegiance to Russia. They dedicated themselves to fighting off what they saw as an "imperialist invasion." ∎

The Alliances That Divided Europe

On the eve of the Great War, Europe was divided into two armed camps: one was the Triple Alliance of Germany, Italy, and Austria-Hungary. And the other was the Triple Entente made up of Russia, Great Britain, and France.

When the war began, the German Empire (the Triple Alliance) was pitted against the Triple Entente.

Germany and its allies soon became known as the Central Powers, because of their location in Europe. The Triple Entente—the rest of Europe and Russia—became known as the Allies. (Italy joined the Allies in 1915.)

Allies	Central Powers
Russia	Germany
Great Britain	Austria-Hungary
France	Bulgaria
Italy	Turkey
United States	
Serbia	
Greece	
Japan	
Montenegro	
Portugal	
Romania	

From Belgium to Turkey

A Trail of Death and Destruction

Belgium: War's First Victim (August 1914)—The ill-prepared, ragtag Belgian army fought bravely, but could not stop the German army. Before most of the world even knew the war had begun, the Germans had burned down the Belgian village of Lise. "They had set light not to a village, but a world," an observer wrote of the German action.

Next the Germans took Liege, an old military fortress that was sorely vulnerable to the world's modern, high-powered guns. By August 20, Brussels, Belgium's capital, had fallen. The Germans were now within reach of France. In the first month of war, nearly 50,000 civilians and soldiers had been killed.

Allied Disaster at Gallipoli (1915-1916)—The Western Front was only one arena of the Great War. Russia and Germany were fighting on the Eastern Front. In the south, France and Great Britain hoped to weaken the Central Powers. They planned to overrun Turkey and take its capital, Constantinople. From the standpoint of strategy, the Gallipoli campaign was a stroke of genius. If it had succeeded, the Allies might have broken the Central Powers in the south.

The battle began on February 19, 1915. British and French battleships fired on Turkish forts along the Gallipoli Peninsula, the entryway to Constantinople. But the Turkish defense, put in place by the Germans, was stronger than the Allies expected. For a year the two powers fought for Gallipoli. By January 1916, the Allies had lost. In humiliation they evacuated their troops. A half-million soldiers and civilians had died. Six battleships were lost.

A Long Bloody Year—1916

When war broke out in 1914, no one believed that it still would be raging 18 months later. But it was. And 1916 is remembered as the worst year of the war. When that year was over, the Allies had lost nearly a million-and-a-half soldiers.

By this point in the war, soldiers as well as civilians on both sides were weary. One in ten Europeans was now fighting the war. And those at home were working to supply their countries with guns and machinery.

The situation was severe in Germany. In December the German government asked President Woodrow Wilson to pass a note proposing peace talks to the Allies. The Allies rejected the German proposal. They wanted more specific information as to how the peace would be organized. Would the Germans retreat? In response, the German command rejected the Allies' request. The Great War's end was nowhere in sight.

Battle of Verdun

French soldiers in the Argonne Forest outside Verdun, preparing to fight off yet another German attack.

The German army (above) marched across the French countryside in early 1916. Its destination was Verdun, a French village near the German-occupied region of Alsace. The Germans hoped that Verdun would be a turning point in the war. Their victory would demoralize the Allied army and force it to surrender. "They shall not pass!" became the French battle cry.

And the German army did not pass. They were stopped within four miles of the town. The Germans dug in; the French counterattacked. For five months the Battle of Verdun raged on. It ended in a stalemate. The French had suffered more that 540,000 casualties, the Germans more than 430,000.

New Sights, Smells, Sounds

The Look of War

Trench Warfare

In the French countryside, the world was exposed to methods of warfare it had never seen before. The soldiers at right illustrate trench warfare—the most common form of "hand-to-hand" combat. Until the Battle of the Marne in 1914, warring armies had faced each other only on the battlefield. They simply charged on foot with their guns firing. But in the Great War, soldiers stood in trenches and fired from behind the protection of earthen mounds. Often more than a mile in length, these trenches came to offer as much danger as they did protection. Soldiers on both sides began to fall victim to illness and disease. The sickness was caused by standing so close together for such a long time in holes filled with cold water.

Poison Gas

In April 1915, at the Battle of Ypres, the German army used the most hideous weapon ever developed. It was an invisible killer: poison gas. Only gas masks, as the men here are wearing, protected soldiers from the deadly new "bomb." Poison gas burned the skin and the eyes, and left soldiers paralyzed and lung-damaged. It even caused death. One observer wrote that poison gas was a "horrible device" that "shook (the Allies) by the physical torture it caused, and by the pain (felt by) those who died." Within six weeks, the Allies had developed their own arsenal of poison gas.

Armored Tanks

Germany had toyed with the idea of developing the tank before the war began. But it was Great Britain that first developed and used tanks, at the urging of Winston Churchill, the naval commander. Called "iron monsters," the first tanks were used by the British along the Somme front. Their effect upon the Germans was profound. There were reports that the German soldiers "panicked" at the sight of the rolling arsenals.

Submarines

Great Britain entered the war as the world's greatest naval power. But Germany emerged as the power behind the submarine—the most deadly military vessel. From the earliest days of the war, German submarines successfully pursued and destroyed scores of Allied cruisers. On one day alone in 1914, German submarines sank three British battleships, killing 1,473 men. And the Germans didn't stop at sinking warships. They also attacked commercial and passenger ships—without warning. One of those sunk was the British passenger liner *Lusitania*. Nearly 1,200 people, including 128 Americans, lost their lives on the *Lusitania*.

In one three-week period in 1917, German submarines sank 134 noncombat vessels, an average of six ships a day. In February 1917, Germany declared "total" submarine warfare on all ships, military or not. It was this declaration that directly led to America's entry into the Great War in Europe.

Airships and Airplanes

On Christmas Day, 1914, residents of a small British village saw the future of warfare: German airplanes were being chased by their British counterparts. In the beginning, though, both sides fought the air war with dirigibles, or zeppelins, as they were commonly called. The Germans used the huge airships to destroy train depots, ammunition factories, and civilian landmarks in France and Great Britain. By 1917, zeppelins had become easy targets for anti-aircraft guns. Much smaller, faster, more maneuverable airplanes—loaded with machine guns, then bombs—took their place. Throughout the winter of 1917–18, the war was "brought home to every Londoner" as German airplanes regularly bombed the city.

America Enters the War

Millions of Men Called to Service

April 6, 1917—The United States today declared war on Germany. In so doing, it formally abandoned its position as "the greatest neutral nation" in the world.

President Woodrow Wilson signed the declaration of war at 1:18 P.M. The resolution was signed without ceremony and in the presence of only the president's family. Word was flashed immediately to all Army and Navy stations, and to vessels at sea.

Until this year, Wilson had strongly argued that the United States remain neutral in the European conflict. But four days ago he urged Congress to pass the war resolution. He cited Germany's "cruel and unmanly business" of submarine warfare against American passenger and commercial ships.

"The world must be made safe for democracy," the president told the Congress. He urged the Senate and House of Representatives to approve the resolution declaring "the existence of a state of war." Both Congressional houses did so in overwhelming numbers.

Warfare Against Mankind

"The present German submarine warfare against commerce is a warfare against mankind. It is a war against all nations," the president said in his speech.

Even as the president spoke, American ships were being sunk by German subs. The steamer *Missourian* was lost in the Atlantic Ocean just the day before.

With the declaration of war, Congress was asked to immediately provide $3.5 billion to finance the Army and Navy for the remainder of the year. The Navy announced that it had contracts out for approximately 200 submarine chasers.

German Ships Seized

The War Department revealed plans for raising an army of men numbering "in the millions" to fight the war in Europe.

Since yesterday, port authorities, including those in San Francisco and New York, have seized 79 German ships. Orders were sent out by the federal government to arrest "dangerous aliens," including former German Consul General Franz Bopp. Bopp was last seen leaving his home in Berkeley, California, yesterday for an automobile trip. His whereabouts are unknown.

Yesterday the government dropped its plans to confine all German citizens living in the United States to detention camps. Only those aliens known to have taken part in plots against the United States were ordered to be arrested.

"We have no quarrel with the German people," President Wilson said in response to the detention camp proposal. "Most of them" are "true and loyal Americans," he added. ⇨

Navy recruiting posters urged Americans to get behind the war effort.

"The world must be made safe for democracy," the president told the Congress.

Some Americans, including many pacifists, denounced the war with Germany. But most stood behind the government's decision. It was to be, President Wilson said, "the war that would end all wars." To show patriotism, cities across the nation held parades, such as New York City's grand display pictured on page 20. The war was expected to require upwards of five million soldiers. And to this end President Wilson (below) drew the names of the first men to be drafted into the Army. The draft was legalized under the Selective Draft Act, which was signed into law May 18, 1917. In the first month of war, three million men were drafted and sent to Europe. One million men volunteered to go. By the end of June, American troops had arrived in France. They were led by Major General John J. "Black Jack" Pershing. In the photograph at right friends and family say goodbye to a group of departing American soldiers. ■

Miss Rankin Bows Head: Cannot Support the War

Jeanette Rankin of Montana, the first woman member of Congress, took her seat in the House of Representatives on April 1, 1917. She was cheered by her male colleagues, and congratulated by feminists and suffragists around the world. Her supporters included Carrie Chapman Catt, president of the National American Women Suffrage Association.

"I want you to know how much I feel this responsibility," Miss Rankin said shortly before entering the House chambers. "There will be many times when I shall make mistakes. And it means a great deal to me to know that I have your encouragement and support." An outburst of applause greeted Miss Rankin when her name was first called on the roll.

Four days later, on April 5, Jeanette Rankin bowed her head when her name was called out by the clerk. Sinking back into her seat, she did not answer his question until the second roll was called. Then she rose and said in a sobbing voice, "I want to stand by my country. But I cannot vote for war."

She stood there for a moment without speaking, as cries of "Vote, Vote" came from several parts of the chamber. But she sat down again in her chair and did not audibly vote. Her vote was then officially recorded in the negative.

A pacifist, Miss Rankin was one of 50 House members to vote against entering the war against Germany.

A Year of Change—1917

Two major events shaped the Great War's progress in 1917. America entered the war in April. And in November, after eight months of internal struggle, the Russian government was seized by antiwar forces. A Communist regime dedicated to world peace took control (see story page 35).

For Germany and the Central Powers, America's entry into the war meant a second wave of Allied troops. These Americans had not been worn down by three years of fighting. America's soldiers were fresh and strong. The Allies had gained needed momentum.

When the Russian leadership changed hands, the Central Powers had something to cheer about. In December the new Russian government pulled the country out of the war. With that move, Germany had won the long battle for the Eastern Front. A triumphant Kaiser Wilhelm proclaimed, "All of Germany fights for her future."

As 1918 dawned, both sides smelled victory. The Germans were ready to make a final push against the French. The allies were prepared for a defense and counterattack. The War had reached a turning point.

Here, American troops crowd a barracks in Beauval, France. Although their supplies appear to be few, the cost of outfitting a "doughboy" in 1917 was a whopping $156.30. That included $2.15 for a bayonet, $3 for a steel helmet, $12 for a gas mask, $19.50 for a rifle, and 98¢ for a bedsack.

The German Eighteenth Army (above) overruns the Allies at the Somme in April 1918. At right, Allied forces machine gun German troops in the Argonne forest.

The Final Battle Rages—1918

From both the north and south the German troops pushed into France in the spring of 1918. First they defeated the Allies along the embattled Somme (above). Then they recaptured lost ground. The German army pushed as far west as the Marne River where it had been in 1914. Already German planes had bombed Paris, killing 13 civilians. Shock waves ran through all the Allied nations.

"I will fight in Paris, I will fight behind Paris. We shall be victorious if the public authorities are equal to their task," cried French Premier Georges Clemenceau. It seemed as if the end was near and the Allies had already been defeated.

Then the first Americans arrived in the early summer. And in July the reinforced Allies launched their counterattack against Germany's advances on the Western Front. The battles in France raged on. Losses were heavy on both sides. "The wheatfields were plowed with bodies," an eyewitness said. American losses were running at 40 percent. In the battle of Belleau Wood, America lost 7,800 men.

By the end of July, the stalemate had been broken. Now the Allies were winning. Battles like those in the Argonne forest (pictured here)— with the Allies using machine guns and cannon fire—helped to turn the tide. But in the end it was the sheer number of Allied troops that had won the war. Reports had come in that the German army was so depleted that it used old men and young boys as recruits. "We cannot get a substitute for men," said a German advisor.

The Tide Turns

By September, the Allied troops had broken through the Austro-Hungarian defense in the south. Now there was nothing left for the Germans. On October 14, 1918, Kaiser Wilhelm sent word to the Allies that the Central Powers would accept a "peace with honor." The Allies said no. As in 1916, the Allies wanted assurances that if the peace were accepted, German troops would withdraw. And there were hints that the Allies also wanted, as part of the peace agreement, the abdication of Kaiser Wilhelm himself. ∎

Peace in Europe Comes in Stages

One by one the Central Powers fell to the Allied forces in the fall of 1918. Bulgaria and Turkey were forced to sign armistices with the Allies in October. In the same month the Allies split and destroyed the Austro-Hungarian armies. In early November, the entire Austro-Hungarian empire crumbled. The Hungarians, Czechs, Slovaks, and Poles declared their independence. On November 3, Emperor Charles I, a ruler without an empire, agreed to an armistice. Nine days later he stepped down.

The last Central Power to sue for peace was Germany. With its people angry and hungry, and its soldiers in revolt, the German government agreed to the Allies' terms. Four days after Wilhelm gave up his throne, representatives of the new German republic and the Allies met. And at 5:00 A.M. on November 11, 1918, the final armistice was signed in a railway car in a French forest. The Great War had finally ended.

The Great War's Victims

The Great War of 1914–1918 was the world's bloodiest war ever. Nearly nine million soldiers died—practically an entire generation was wiped out.

Worse, the war knew no boundaries. Millions of civilians fell victim to the conflict as the Allied and Central Powers' forces raged across Europe. Nearly five million civilians died in areas where the war was fought. Starvation, disease, and exposure were responsible for most of these deaths.

In addition, the Spanish influenza epidemic that had been sweeping the world claimed millions of more lives by the end of 1918. And when peace finally came to war-torn Europe, most of its countries were threatened by severe food shortages.

The Toll

Allied Powers

- **Belgium:** 13,716 dead; 44,686 wounded; 34,659 prisoners or missing.

- **British** Empire: 908,371 dead; 2 million wounded; 197,652 prisoners or missing.

- **France:** 1.3 million dead; 4.2 million wounded; 537,000 prisoners or missing.

- **Russia:** 1.7 million dead; 4.9 million wounded; 2.5 million prisoners or missing.

- **U.S.:** 116,516 dead; 204,002 wounded; 4,500 prisoners or missing.

- **Total** (including casualities reported by Greece, Italy, Japan, Montenegro, Portugal, Romania, and Serbia): 5.1 million dead; 12 million wounded; 4.1 million prisoners or missing.

Central Powers

- **Austria-Hungary:** 1.2 million dead; 3.6 million wounded; 2.2 million prisoners or missing.

- **Germany:** 1.7 million dead; 4.2 million wounded; 1.1 million prisoners or missing.

- **Total** (including casualties reported by Bulgaria and Turkey): 3.3 million dead; 8.3 million wounded; 3.6 million prisoners or missing.

Total, both sides

- 8.4 million dead; 20.3 million wounded; 7.7 million prisoners or missing.

Wounded Americans wait for a field ambulance to take them to a base hospital.

Royal Families Chased from Their Castles

Wilhelm Abdicates

The war had lost its support among the German people long before the surprise Allied victory.

Germans were demoralized and discouraged by the war's impact on daily life. In November 1918, a key fact became obvious to the German government and its military. The country's salvation seemed tied to the Allies' unspoken demand: Kaiser Wilhem II, emperor of Germany, must give up his throne.

Two weeks after the kaiser forwarded his unaccepted plea for "peace with honor," he secretly left Berlin. Wilhem feared a revolt of his own soldiers, and his fears were well founded. On November 4, the navy at Kiel, Germany, mutinied. The sailors who revolted set up councils similar to those of the Bolsheviks' in Russia (see page 33). Joined by socialists, they called for the kaiser's abdication and the creation of a German republic.

On November 9, Wilhem stepped down from the throne and fled to Holland. Two days later, Austro-Hungarian ruler, Emperor Charles I also sought refuge in Holland. Throughout the German Empire, royalty fled as the people revolted against their autocratic leaders. The Duke of Brunswick and five other kings, princes, and grand dukes were chased from their castles by angry demonstrators. In Holland, an assassin shot and killed Count Stephen Tisza, the former Hungarian premier. "The hour of reckoning has come," the assassin said as he fired three shots from his rifle. ∎

The Dancer Who Was a Spy

She was born Margaretha Gertrud Zelle, but the world came to know her best as Mata Hari. On October 15, 1917, she was shot by a French firing squad. She had been found guilty of spying against the Allies.

Tall and beautiful, Margaretha Zelle was born in the Netherlands in 1876. She came to Paris in 1905 after having lived for years in Malaysia. She soon changed her name to "Mata Hari"— a Malay expression for the sun—and became an exotic dancer. For the next several years she was very popular in Paris and other European cities.

During the war, Mata Hari became very well acquainted with military officers on both sides. In February 1917 she was arrested in Paris. The French accused her of agreeing to spy for the Germans while she had been living in Holland the year before. She was tried by a French military court in July 1917, found guilty, and sentenced to death. Neither the evidence against her, nor the information she supposedly supplied to the Germans, was ever revealed by the French government.

Mata Hari was escorted to the firing squad by two nuns and a priest.

Mata Hari

To the Victors Go the Spoils

Peace came exactly five years to the day after the assassination of Archduke Ferdinand. On June 28, 1919, five separate treaties were signed at Versailles, France, by the victorious Allies and the defeated Central Powers.

The terms of the peace were harsh. There was no pity among the Allies, especially for the Germans. The Treaty of Versailles said that the German government was solely responsible for the war. The treaty forbade Germany from manufacturing weapons. It forced the German government to abolish its navy, and said that it could raise an army of no more than 100,000 men.

The most controversial terms of the peace agreements were those that dealt with territories held by the Central Powers. Even before the meeting in Versailles, the Allies had made secret deals with each other. They had already decided how to divide up postwar Europe and the Middle East. Now the losers in the war stood by helplessly as the victors redrew the map of Europe to their own advantages.

Germany, Turkey and Austria-Hungary lost, in total, nearly half the land they once held. Germany even had to return portions of France that it had acquired in the late 1800s.

New countries were born out of fallen empires and defeated nations. The Austro-Hungarian Empire became three separate independent nations: Austria, Hungary, and Czechoslovakia. Territories from Austria, Germany, and Russia were combined to form a new Poland. Portions of Austria-Hungary, Bulgaria, and Montenegro were added to Serbia to form Yugoslavia. The defeated nations also lost territories in the Middle East and Africa. ∎

The "Big Three" at Paris

The Paris Peace Conference began as a meeting of all nations involved in the Great War. But it ended with three men in control—the "Big Three" as they were called. They were French Premier Georges Clemenceau, British Prime Minister David Lloyd George, and United States President Woodrow Wilson.

Wilson was a popular figure in Europe. America's joining the Allies had helped end the war. In 1918 Wilson had come up with the Fourteen Points, a revolutionary way of "world thinking." Among the points was a call for a world body to peacefully settle disputes between nations. And it was this *League of Nations* that was established as part of the peace agreement.

For war-weary Europeans, Wilson's plan was a breath of fresh air, a hopeful program for the future. Everywhere he went, Wilson was cheered as a hero. But as popular as Wilson was, he didn't have the real power at the conference. That distinction went to French Premier Clemenceau. The French leader, nicknamed the "Tiger," was the force behind many of the Allies' demands. His goal was to hurt and humiliate Germany in peace as it had hurt and humiliated France in battle. When the conference ended, many people felt that he had succeeded.

Allied Leaders at the Peace Conference—Seated (from left) Italian Premier Vittorio Orlando, and the "Big Three": British Prime Minister David Lloyd George, French Premier Georges Clemenceau, and U.S. President Woodrow Wilson.

A 300-Year Dynasty Falls

The Russian people blamed the tsar and his ministers for their troubles.

"What is to become of me? I know nothing of the business of ruling." Thus spoke Nicholas Romanov, at the time he became tsar of Russia in 1894, when his father died.

Twenty-three years later, the Russian people came to agree with Nicholas. In March 1917, after years of trouble and turmoil, Nicholas II was forced to give up his throne. His stepping down ended the 300-year-old Romanov dynasty in Russia.

For years the Russian people had been dissatisfied with the ruling family. The country's disastrous war with Japan in 1904–05 left many Russians angry and humiliated. They blamed the tsar and his ministers for the defeat.

The revolution of 1905 forced Nicholas to grant his people a representative form of government. But the Duma, as the national assembly was named, was powerless. Control of the empire never left the tsar's hands.

Perhaps the unhappiest people in Russia were the peasants. These people, called serfs, made up nearly 85 percent of the country's population. They had been slaves until they were freed by the Emancipation of 1861. But that document didn't make the serfs totally free. Fifty years later their poverty still tied them to their wealthy landlords. Very few were allowed to own land of their own.

It was well known that Nicholas Romanov would rather not have been tsar in these troublesome times. He was happiest when he was hunting, or at home with his family. He was very close to his wife, Alexandra, and their five children. But when his father died, Nicholas was forced by tradition to take the reins of government.

The beginning of the end of the Romanov dynasty came in August 1914. That month Tsar Nicholas declared war against Germany. He made this unpopular move in spite of the unrest with his rule.

Tsar Nicholas, last of the Romanov rulers.

For a decade Russia's cities had been disabled by strikes. Factory workers were emerging as the country's newest social class. These workers demanded better wages and working conditions.

New political parties, notably the socialists, came out of this unrest. The socialists' most ambitious wing was the revolutionary Bolshevik party. Its founder and leader was named Vladimir Ilyich Lenin. Its goal was the total overthrow of Russia's monarchy and the establishment of a worker's state.

The tsar's government no longer inspired loyalty among the country's huge peasant class. The mass of the peasants pledged no allegiance to the Russian "nation." They were loyal to their individual nationalities, among them Ukranian, Armenian, and Georgian. The call to war made many people angry. The 15 million men eventually sent to fight would come mainly from the peasant class.

Not Enough Food or Boots

Nicholas also overestimated his nation's strength. And he stubbornly refused to reconsider his decision or listen to his people's complaints. When war began, Russia had less than half the guns and ammunition needed to equip its army. It did not have enough food or boots to give its men. People inside both Russia and Europe saw Nicholas as a poor commander. And they agreed that the tsar's advisers in the war were the least talented men in his government. They also did not trust the tsar's closest adviser, his wife, Alexandra.

Alexandra was born a German princess. When she married Nicholas in 1894, she had embraced Russia as well as its orthodox religion. But she inspired little love among the Russian people. Alexandra was said to be "cold." As time went on, stories about her spread among the people. Many of these stories concerned her relationship with a bearded, poorly dressed, often unwashed, "holy man" named Rasputin. (See box on page 31.) There were even some who claimed that Alexandra was a spy for the German enemy. However, evidence to prove that charge was never found. ■

The Tsar Leads the Troops

By the winter of 1917, Russia had lost six million men in the Great War. The Russian war effort was so disorganized that the majority of Russian soldiers now fought without guns. What guns they had were taken from their fallen countrymen or dead Germans. They also took the Germans' boots, for Russia had none to give its men.

So unskilled were Nicholas's generals that many of the men deserted. And many of the deserters joined the growing ranks of the Bolsheviks. Organizers for the Bolsheviks had gone into the army looking for recruits for their cause. Peace with Germany and land reform were the Bolshevik slogans. Both ideas greatly appealed to soldiers and peasants alike.

Two years earlier, in 1915, Nicholas himself had gone to war. He had hoped his presence would inspire the army. But it was a futile gesture. It made matters worse, in fact, because Nicholas had turned over the government to Alexandra. And through her, control of the government went to Rasputin. "Be my eyes and ears in the capital while I'm away," the tsar had said to his wife.

.... the majority of Russian soldiers now fought without guns.

They had said their farewells at their palace outside Petrograd.

That year, in a fit of wartime pride, the capital city had been renamed. Since the war, anti-German feelings were strong. So, the government decided the capital should be changed from the German-sounding "St. Petersburg" to its Russian name, Petrograd.

During Nicholas's time in the army, conditions at home worsened. In February 1917, temperatures in Petrograd were well below freezing. But there was not enough coal or firewood for the people. There was no bread. Food in general was in short supply. And what was available cost far more than most Russians could afford. Yet the tsarina paid no heed to these conditions. She rarely mentioned the chaos in letters to her "darling Nicky." Alexandra and her friends at court lived in a separate world. A British visitor remarked that the wealthy classes were clothed in a "richness and extravagance (that) went oddly in company with a distressed and impoverished Russia." ■

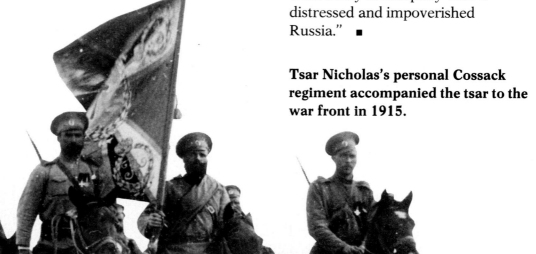

Tsar Nicholas's personal Cossack regiment accompanied the tsar to the war front in 1915.

"Rasputin—The Holy Devil"

In the Russian language, the word "rasputin" means degenerate, or evil. Rasputin was also the name of a longhaired, shaggy-bearded, foul-mouthed monk who called himself a holy man. To many Russians, he was, indeed, the perfect example of a degenerate. From the time he came to St. Petersburg, there were rumors about him. It was said that Rasputin was involved in a number of shady schemes and immoral affairs.

Rasputin claimed to be a Siberian "starets." That was what the Russians called a holy man who roamed the countryside in voluntary poverty. But Rasputin was not satisfied with being a wandering holy man. His sights were set higher. It was the royal family he wanted to influence with his supposed supernatural powers. And the one person he especially wanted to get close to was the tsarina.

Tsarina Alexandra was an easy target for a man like Rasputin. She was a firm believer in the supernatural. For her, it was the only answer to the most tragic "problem" in her life. And that problem was the ill health of her only son.

The Tsarevich Alexi was the heir to the Romanov throne. The young man suffered from hemophilia, an inherited blood disease that threatened his life each day. Young Alexi was unable to have any kind of a normal childhood because of his disease. The slightest bruise could cause internal bleeding. And if the bleeding was not stopped, he could die.

Alexi had had numerous close calls. One time the palace doctor stood by helplessly, unable to stop the boy's bleeding. Then Rasputin supposedly used his "power of prayer" to pull the boy back from death's grasp. That act convinced the tsarina of Rasputin's "holiness."

From that point on, Rasputin rarely left the palace. He grew more and more important to the royal family. Unfortunately, for both Rasputin and the Romanovs, he did not limit his interest to the family's personal life. He began advising the tsar about Russia's government and policies.

The people of Russia had gossiped for years about Rasputin's influence on the tsarina. Most often his power was described as "magnetic." Some said his eyes "willed" a person to do his bidding. So when Rasputin started advising the tsar on the war, other members of the tsar's own family stepped in. They took matters into their own hands.

Rasputin, they said, was worse than a fake. Now he was a danger to the country as well.

On December 29, 1916, a young prince invited Rasputin to his home. The young man was married to the tsar's niece. He had promised Rasputin food, drink, and entertainment. Instead, the prince and two friends planned to kill him.

First they put poison in his wine. Rasputin drank several glasses. But the poison had no effect. Then one of them shot Rasputin in the heart. But still he lived, crawling toward them, growling and cursing. Finally, they fired into his body until the gun was empty. When Rasputin at last lay still, the three men took him to the river. They cut a hole in the ice, and threw the body in.

Three days later the body was found. An autopsy showed that neither the poison nor the bullets had killed Rasputin. He had drowned.

None of the young men involved were arrested, though their names were known. ∎

Gregory Rasputin, the tsarina's adviser and close friend.

"Long Live the Revolution!"

"Down with the Tsar"

Nicholas Romanov's reign met its fate on International Women's Day, March 8, 1917. The day was being celebrated as a Russian holiday honoring the working woman. Women were out on the streets protesting in Moscow and Petrograd. Many carried signs that read "Bread" and "Peace." That day, too, Petrograd workers were striking for better wages and working conditions.

The strikes grew, and the demonstrators' numbers increased steadily over the next few days. They were aided by political organizing among the Bolsheviks. New banners read: "Down with the Tsar!" and "Long Live the Revolution!" But there was still no word of reform from Nicholas.

Instead, the tsar's guards were sent out to control the crowd. Nicholas had even issued orders to open fire when necessary. The monarchy was startled at the reaction to that order—the royal guards, soldiers, and sailors refused to fight their countrymen. Instead, they *joined* the demonstrators' revolt. Their decision to join the uprising was the turning point in the March Revolution.

Four days later, on March 12, Nicholas's government fell. Demonstrators occupied the Fortress of Peter and Paul in Petrograd. It was the seat of the tsar's government. Then the revolution spread to Moscow and other large cities. Soon from all quarters the Russian people demanded that Nicholas step down. Even his advisers thought it wise. They begged Nicholas to turn the government over to his brother, Grand Duke Mikhail. "Do not delay," one of Nicholas's advisers said to the tsar. "The hour that will decide your fate and that of our homeland has come. Tomorrow it may be too late."

Three days later, after repeatedly refusing to do so, Nicholas Romanov gave in. "I have decided. I shall renounce the throne," he said to an aide. He then signed the abdication proclamation. The reign of Nicholas II was over. Its end came suddenly and without much bloodshed. One hundred sixty-nine people died in the revolution that completely changed the face of old Russia. The 300-year-old monarchy crumbled when Mikhail refused to succeed his brother.

After stepping down from the throne, Nicholas was put under house arrest along with Alexandra and their children. They were held at their palace, Tsarskoe Selo. In 1918 they were moved to Ekaterinburg in Siberia. And on July 16 of that year, all seven were executed by several unnamed Bolshevik assassins. ∎

After the tsar's government fell, power passed to the national parliament, the Duma, which formed Russia's new Provisional Government.

Alexander Kerensky (standing, top left) was Prime Minister and Minister of War in the new Provisional Government.

Kerensky Takes Control

The government that took control from the tsar was headed by a moderate socialist named Alexander Kerensky. The new government was put together quickly, for Russia was still at war. And the problems that sparked the March Revolution still plagued the country. The people were still demanding more food, land reform, and better working conditions.

Kerensky's government represented several left-wing political groups that were competing for power in the new Russia. The only one missing was the Bolshevik party. Lenin, its leader, was in Switzerland. He had lived there off and on since his exile by the tsar.

Although a minority party, the Bolsheviks were a strong and growing force. They organized outside the newly assembled Provisional Government, which they did not support. The Bolshevik strength was being established in the "soviets." These were unions of workers that had been formed in Petrograd, Moscow, and other industrial cities.

Peace was what most Russians wanted from their new government. But Kerensky's hands were tied. His government was too disorganized and inexperienced to quickly turn the country around. Nor did he want to anger Russia's allies by abandoning the fight. At this point in

time, friendly allies were important to the young and struggling government. More Russians were killed as the war raged on. The people grumbled louder. The new government was on shaky ground.

In April 1917, Lenin was smuggled onto a train (some say by the Germans) and returned to Petrograd in triumph. For the next six months he campaigned and led demonstrations against the Kerensky government. He built up his political base by promising to end the war if his party came to power. The slower the new government was to institute reforms, the faster Lenin's influence grew. "He captured the imagination ⇨

On November 6, 1917, the Russian cruiser *Aurora* sailed into Petrograd flying a red flag showing full support for the Bolshevik attempt to seize power. Here, sailors from the ship keep order with fixed bayonets in the city streets.

> The takeover was so clean and simple it astounded everyone, including Lenin.

of the people," an observer wrote of Lenin. His Bolshevik party also gained new followers. In October of that year, there were elections in the Petrograd and Moscow soviets. The results gave the Bolsheviks a leading edge.

Changing of the Guard

On November 7, 1917, Lenin got the opportunity to make good his promise of peace. That night in Petrograd the Bolsheviks occupied the Winter Palace, the seat of Kerensky's government. His deputies resigned immediately and almost without a fight. There was only "a brief exchange of fire." And with the help of government sailors and soldiers, Lenin now became Russia's third leader in a year. This time, however, the changeover created the world's first Communist nation.

"It was less like an insurrection than a changing of the guard," said a Russian statesman. Only 20 people were killed. The takeover was so clean and simple it astounded everyone, including Lenin. When it was all over, Lenin turned to his second-in-command, Leon Trotsky, and said, "It makes one dizzy." ∎

"Ivan Speaks"

Between 1915 and 1917 a Russian nurse named Madame Fedorchenko wrote down the conversations she had and over-heard with Russian soldiers at the front.

They talked of the tsar and their duty as soldiers. They spoke of their families and memories of happier days. Most often, though, they told of the terror of war.

"Oh, yes, it hurts when you get wounded! But you get over it, and live on. You eat and drink and talk to people, and are again a man among other men. But the poison gases! To pay for those, many, many Germans should be killed. Nothing could be worse than gas. It twists you and tortures the soul out of you. You won't ever be glad again, not for one little hour."

A Note About Dates

On February 1, 1918, the Bolsheviks abolished the Julian calendar used by the tsar and the Russian Orthodox church. They replaced it with the Gregorian calendar used in most of the world. The Julian calendar was 13 days behind the Gregorian calendar.

All dates in this text follow the Gregorian calendar.

Ukraine Is Lost

Lenin Makes Peace

As he had promised, Lenin immediately declared that Russia was at peace with Germany. The next month he met with the Kaiser's representatives to work out the peace treaty. In return for an end to the fighting, Germany made some demands. Russia was forced to give up the Ukraine, among other territories. It was a sore loss. The Ukraine was the country's major agricultural area. Many called it Russia's "bread basket."

Along with peace, Lenin also made good his promise of land reform. He simply gave the land to the peasants. To do so he took away and divided up estates owned by Russia's wealthy landowners. Lenin's party also seized banks and industries. In addition, the Bolsheviks refused to pay the tsar's outstanding debts to the Allies. All these actions made bitter enemies of Russia's former allies and other non-Communists inside Russia.

By the spring of 1918, the European countries and the United States were openly anti-Bolshevik. Before the end of the year, the Allies landed thousands of troops on Russian soil. Their aim was to support the anti-Bolshevik forces inside Russia.

These forces, called the "White Army," engaged the Bolshevik Red Army in numerous battles. The fighting finally erupted into a full-scale civil war. And the struggle for control of the Russian government was still continuing at the end of the decade. ■

Lenin's Proclamations

Along with peace and land reform, the Bolshevik government made several other proclamations in November 1917. These included:

- Abolition of all titles and class divisions, both civilian and military.

- Expansion of women's rights.

- Liberalization of divorce laws.

- Revision of the Russian alphabet.

Vladimir Lenin, leader of the world's first communist nation.

Flu Epidemic Wipes Out Millions

November 1918 brought an end to the war in Europe, but it also brought a horrible health crisis—to the entire world. It was an epidemic of "Spanish" influenza, or flu. And it spread like a wildfire to every corner of the globe.

No cure was ever found. The "bug"—whatever it was—had virtually disappeared by the end of the decade. But by then the flu epidemic was responsible for more than 20 million deaths worldwide. That is two-and-one-half times more than all the people killed in four years of the Great War.

Many medical professionals believe that the epidemic got started at Fort Riley, Kansas. There, in March 1918, more than one hundred soldiers in training came down with the sickness. All of them had the same symptoms: high fever, sore throat, headache, and muscular pains.

The troops at Fort Riley lived in crowded, somewhat unhealthy conditions. All across the country, America's military posts were in similar shape. Overcrowding couldn't be avoided: thousands and thousands of U.S. servicemen were being prepared for overseas duty in the Great War.

In May, troops from Fort Riley were shipped to France. But by that time more than 1,100 soldiers had been stricken and 46 had died. Within weeks of the troops' arrival in France, new cases of the flu were being reported around the country. Before long, the epidemic was sweeping across all of Europe.

At the same time the epidemic had somehow spread to Asia. It rolled over China and Japan "like a tidal wave," according to a doctor from the Shanghai Health Department. Had the outbreak in Asia originated there? Or had it been imported from Europe or the United States? No one was really sure.

Why did so many people die? One reason was that the disease caused great damage to a victim's lungs. Hemorrhaging, pneumonia, bronchitis, and even complete lung collapse were caused by the flu virus.

Another reason that so many died was that the disease was *very* contagious. People everywhere went to great lengths to avoid contacting the germs. Street sweepers, barbers, and thousands of other workers wore face masks to ward off germs. In some cities, *anyone* appearing in the street without a mask was subject to arrest. Victims were kept isolated from the general population until they either recovered—or died. Still the epidemic continued to spread.

Hospitals around the world were unable to handle the huge number of cases. Many cities set up outdoor "tent hospitals." These makeshift hospitals helped handle the extra cases and gave the patients much needed fresh air and sunshine.

By 1919 the worst of the epidemic seemed to be over. But the final number of fatalities is enormous. In the United States 500,000 people died. In Europe the death toll was also staggering: United Kingdom, 229,000; France, 166,000; Spain, 170,000; Germany, 225,000; Italy, 375,000; and Russia, 450,000. In Japan, 257,000 died, and in India the tragic number of victims was an almost unbelievable 12 million. ∎

American soldiers were told to gargle with salt water to help ward off contamination during the epidemic.

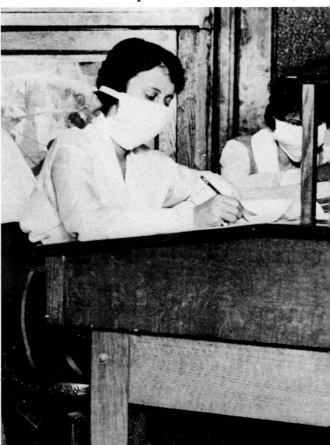

Thousands of workers wore face masks to protect themselves from germs during the worldwide flu epidemic of 1918.

Immigrants in the registration room at Ellis Island, 1912.

America Becomes The Great Melting Pot

"**G**ive me your tired, your poor, your huddled masses yearning to breathe free," read the words engraved on the Statue of Liberty in New York Harbor. When the year 1910 had ended, more than one million people had taken those words to heart and found a new home in the United States. It was the peak year in the wave of immigration that had begun in 1890.

As time went on, the numbers of immigrants swelled the U.S. population. A 30-year total of 18.3 million immigrants had landed on American shores by the end of 1919. Their presence created a new American image, the "great melting pot." The United States became a home for people who represented every nationality in the world. To the immigrants, America was the land of promise. ⇨

Immigration to the United States

Every nation in the world is represented in the wave of immigration that swept across America in the years between 1890 and 1919. See the chart below for statistics.

- **Great Britain:** 1.17 million
- **Ireland:** 917,000
- **Scandinavia** and other northwestern European countries: 1.5 million
- **Germany:** 1.8 million
- **Central Europe,** including Poland: 3.8 million

- **Italy** and other southern European countries: 4.4 million
- **Russia:** 3 million
- **Asian:** 6.3 million
- **Mexico:** 217,000
- **Canada:** 764,000
- **Africa** and **Australia:** 45,000

A street in the Lower East End of New York's Manhattan borough: It became a settlement community for European immigrants.

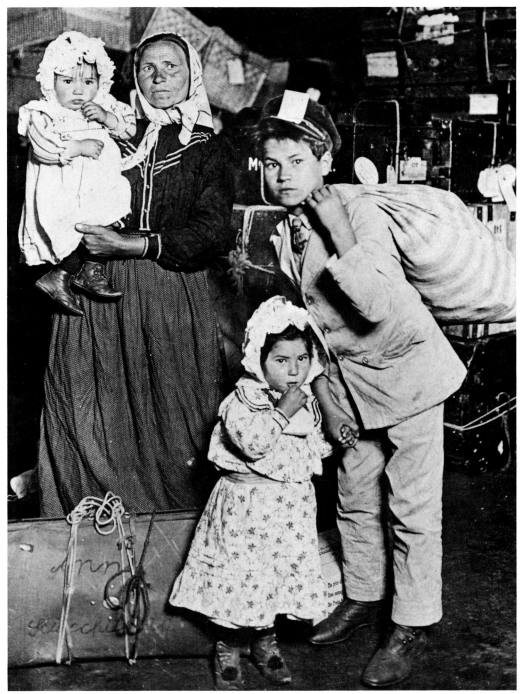

An Italian mother and her three children arrive at the Ellis Island immigration station. This famous photograph was taken by Lewis Hine, a journalist and photographer whose work championed the working men, women, and children of America. Hine's series of photographs of children working in factories helped pass a 1912 law to protect the young.

Not everyone who wanted to stay in America was allowed to do so, however. Some people were turned away because of health reasons. And some were sent back because of criminal charges including polygamy, feeblemindedness and pauperism.

Getting in was not an easy task. There were often delays. For Asian immigrants arriving on the West Coast, for example, there were months of detention before the government could process their papers. The major immigration stations were Ellis Island in New York Harbor and Angel Island in San Francisco Bay.

Some Americans wanted to keep the immigrants out. The most organized anti-immigrationists belonged to the Immigration Restriction League. This organization lobbied for legislation that would officially bar newcomers. Their hope was to set up a literacy test aimed specifically at keeping out southern and eastern Europeans (including Slavs, Jews, and Italians). Literacy-test bills were in fact passed by Congress in 1896, 1909, and 1915. But they were vetoed by presidents Grover Cleveland, William Howard Taft and Woodrow Wilson. For the millions who did settle here, America quickly became home.

Most immigrants chose to stay in cities. Rather than move to rural areas, they made their homes in places like New York, Philadelphia, Chicago, and San Francisco.

United in an "alien" land by language and culture, the immigrants tended to stay together. They moved into neighborhoods that rapidly took on their character. In New York, for example, the Lower East Side was home to European immigrants, and Italians settled in Yonkers. In San Francisco, the Asians found homes in Chinatown, and the Russians moved to the city's Richmond District.

In these neighborhoods, the new Americans could easily find and enjoy the food, entertainment, styles of dress, customs, and religions they had brought with them from the "old world." ∎

Strikes, Strife and Suffragettes

Strikers fight the militia during the Lawrence, Massachusetts, strike of 1912.

Strikes, race riots, antiwar protests, and the "Red Scare," were just a few of the problems Americans faced during the decade. With the addition of antiliquor campaigns, postwar unemployment, and the fight to get women to vote, life at home had plenty of disruptions between 1910 and 1920.

Labor unrest started building between 1912 and 1914, beginning with a 30,000-person walkout in Lawrence, Massachusetts. Workers in the wool and cotton mills there went on strike when the state reduced the workweek for women and children.

The strikers were supported by the country's socialist union organization, the Industrial Workers of the World (I.W.W.), also known as the Wobblies.

Because women and children made up the bulk of the work force, the Lawrence textile employers saved money by reducing hours, while the employees took home less pay. The average wage was 16 cents an hour. The strikers demanded a 15 percent wage increase—or about 2.5 cents more—and double pay for overtime work.

"The strikers, including children as young as 14, have marched abreast through the city streets, forcing other pedestrians off the sidewalks," it was reported. "They have clashed repeatedly with law enforcement officials."

In May 1916, pacifists and Communists demonstrated against America's involvement in the Great War. The men above are protesting the war with picket signs written in English and Russian.

The Lawrence strikers did win a pay increase, though it was not as much as they had demanded. Their success fueled another strike against textile employers. This one took place the following spring in New Hampshire. It was led by the labor leaders involved in Lawrence. But the New Hampshire strike ended in failure. Workers were forced to go back to work without gaining anything.

The worst defeat for labor was yet to come, however. In the fall of 1913, miners in Colorado struck for better working conditions and more pay. Violence, not compromise, was the end result. For months strikers battled with the state militia. Finally, on April 20, 1914, 14 persons were killed in what became known as the "Ludlow Massacre." The mining company, controlled by Rockefeller interests, did not agree to union requests even after the killings. The federal government sent out troops to break the strike.

Although the unions had faced two major defeats in 1913–14, a major victory was won in October 1914. At last Congress passed the Clayton Act, a law that granted organized labor the right to strike and picket.

Labor's Bill of Rights

Among labor and its leaders, the Clayton Act was considered a "new bill of rights." Samuel Gompers, president of the American Federation of Labor, one of the major labor organizations in the nation, best stated the view of workers. He said the act was the Magna Carta for the working man because it recognized that "the labor of a human being is not a commodity or article of commerce."

By 1919, labor unrest reached its boiling point. In that year there were 3,500 strikes across the country. One was a railroad strike that ended only when President Woodrow Wilson agreed to wage increases. Another was a coal miners' strike that also ended when the government stepped in with wage settlements.

One of the worst of the year's strikes occurred in Gary, Indiana. There, 2,000 steel miners walked off the job. Violence broke out when strikers stopped a streetcar taking 40 "strikebreakers" to the steel mills. More than 50 people were injured in the rioting that followed. Federal troops were called in and the city was put under martial law. Charges were made that the strikers were being led by Bolshevik sympathizers.

That year as well, 1,500 police went on strike in Boston, Massachusetts. Like nearly all strikers, they complained of low pay and poor working conditions. The police strike was accompanied by riots in the street, with mobs breaking windows and looting stores. Order was restored by the National Guard. ■

Negroes Protest Racism

As workers struggled for fair treatment, American Negroes launched a campaign of their own. Their protest was against racism and inequality in employment and education. With the founding of the newly renamed National Association for the Advancement of Colored People (NAACP) in 1909, organized protests gained momentum across the country. Racism also increased along with the activism of the Negroes.

One such incident occurred in August 1917, as America was readying its soldiers for war. In Houston, Texas, the quartering of a Negro regiment led to a riot that left 17 persons dead. Thirty-four Negroes were charged with leading the riot. And the state of Texas threatened to send the entire regiment back to its home base at Deming, New Mexico.

The riot began when a Negro soldier saw a white policeman slapping a Negro woman. The soldier objected and was beaten and thrown in jail by the policeman. A Negro officer who went to the police to find out what had happened was also beaten and jailed. When other Negro soldiers heard of the beatings, they shouldered their weapons. Among the victims in the ensuing riot was a 15-year-old girl.

Within two years, race riots had broken out in cities throughout the country. In Norfolk, Virginia, six persons were killed in a riot that erupted when police tried to break up a fight. Several people were killed and nearly 100 injured in riots in Washington, D.C. The NAACP charged that the militia sent out in Washington attacked "innocent and unoffending Negroes."

But the worst riot of the decade occurred in Chicago in the summer of 1919. Thirty-one persons were killed and more than 500 injured in the fighting that raged through the city's South Side. Homes were looted, stores were burned down, and mail delivery was interrupted. Streets became a battle zone with rioters hurling bricks and stones and police officers firing back with shotguns and pistols.

The violence was finally stopped by military troops whose orders stated: "Draw no color line. A white rioter is as dangerous as a Negro rioter." ∎

With the formation of the National Association for the Advancement of Colored People in 1909, Negroes in America began to organize their fight for equality. Parades like this one in New York in 1912 were commonplace.

The Red Scare

Civil unrest did not stop with the race issue. The government of the United States and many private citizens were terrified by the "Red Menace"—U.S. members of the Communist Party. The government pointed a finger at various labor unions, including the Wobblies, as hotbeds of Communist influence.

In January 1920, the Department of Justice authorized raids in 33 American cities. These raids led to the arrest of 3,000 "suspected" Communists. Those arrested were charged with being advocates of "the overthrow of the government by violence and force . . . (who) endeavor to establish a Soviet form of government in this country, similar to that . . . in Russia."

Some members of Congress urged strong penalties, including the death sentence, for those found guilty of Communist party membership. Other voices from Congress said that any foreigners among those arrested should be deported immediately. The justification for their deportation was a law passed in 1918 that prohibited aliens from joining groups "desiring the overthrow of the U.S. government."

Thousands arrested in surprise raids.

In a related move, motion picture executives passed a resolution to fight Communist influence in their industry. They proposed doing "all that is within our power to uphold and strengthen the spirit of 'Americanism' as shown in the movies." ∎

Pacifists and the Unemployed

America's entry in the Great War created two camps of discontent. One group had objected to America's participation in the war from the outset. The other group was made up of those who came back from the war to find themselves unemployed.

When the war began in 1914, America had been a staunch neutral nation. "Isolationists" were in the majority. These included people like President Wilson, automobile tycoon Henry Ford, and many suffragists. All believed that the United States should concentrate on its own "sphere of influence" and stay out of Europe's problems.

Although President Wilson later changed his mind, many Americans did not. Across the nation "pacifists" rallied against mobilization of U.S. troops. American Communists were among those protesting the war.

Jobs in Short Supply

In 1919, the economy was weakened by the expense of the war. And until the economy could adjust itself to "peacetime" industry, jobs were in short supply.

Making matters worse for the returning soldiers were the many women now in the work force. Women had taken many of the jobs vacated by men when they left for war. And women workers were popular among employers. Their wages were much lower than men's. Further, in many cases, women were often banned from membership in labor unions. That meant they were "safe" labor as well—workers who would not go on strike.

The strikes that plagued industry in the postwar years had caused another problem. They had decreased the number of jobs available. On top of that, the economy was shaken by inflation created by "profiteers." These were businessmen who held back commodities in order to get a higher price when demand increased. This practice, called "price gouging," hit hardest at the food industry. In 1919, President Wilson ordered that food being held back by these profiteers be seized from warehouses in Chicago, St. Louis, and Birmingham, Alabama. Wilson also urged that all profiteers be prosecuted. ∎

Jobs were hard to come by in the years after the war ended. Here, men line up in an employment office in Los Angeles. They hope to be among the few lucky ones to find work that day.

Four gentlemen in a saloon down the last "legal" alcoholic beverages before the beginning of Prohibition.

Constitution Makes U.S. "Bone Dry"

Prohibition Begins at Midnight

January 16, 1920—The party is over. Enforcement of the nationwide prohibition against drinking alcoholic beverages—the 18th amendment to the Constitution—begins at 12:01 A.M. tomorrow morning.

"After that hour," a government official said, "not a barrel of intoxicating liquor, a case of wine, or a keg of beer can be legally manufactured, sold, or transported anywhere in the United States."

In the past few months, many Americans have been buying up cases of whiskey and wine. It will still be legal to store liquor at home, where drinking will continue to be ⇨

allowed. Federal authorities say private homes will not be searched.

The latest figures on the impact of the 18th amendment are impressive. These figures show that 236 distilleries, 1,092 breweries, and 177,790 saloons will go out of business.

Most saloons are being turned into restaurants or candy stores, their owners report. Breweries, in many cases, have been turned into malt sugar factories, automobile factories, or meatpacking warehouses. And an "army" of bartenders have found jobs at soda fountains.

Passage of the 18th amendment into law did not come as a surprise. Antiliquor campaigners have been fighting for the Prohibition law for a number of years.

"The false charge is made that Prohibition was 'put over' on the country while American soldiers were fighting in France," said William H. Anderson, a leader of the Anti-Saloon League. "The truth is that in December 1914, the question was voted on in Congress and received a majority in the House of Representatives.

"Prohibition was consummated

> An "army" of bartenders have found jobs at soda fountains.

New York Library Will Not Ban Books On Liquor

Books on the manufacture of alcoholic liquors will continue to be available in the reference department of the New York Public Library, said Edwin H. Anderson.

Anderson said he was surprised by reports that libraries in Massachusetts and Connecticut had removed such books from their shelves. "We would no more think of forbidding readers to consult those books than we would books on flying," he said.

by the moral element in American citizenship," Anderson added. "And that includes the business element which recognized that alcohol, even when moderately used, lessened efficiency."

Anderson also said that antiliquor supporters were active as far back as 1642, when the Maryland colony passed a law punishing drunkenness. ∎

Here's What the "Dry" Law Permits and Forbids

What You Can Do

∎ You can keep the liquor you already have in your home; you can drink it there and serve it to guests.

∎ If you're sick, you can get a doctor's prescription for alcohol-based medicine. The limit is one pint every 10 days.

∎ If you move, you can take your liquor with you, provided you get a permit first.

What You Can't Do

∎ You can't buy a drink anywhere in the United States.

∎ You can't carry a flask on your hip.

∎ You can't drink anywhere except at home or as a "bona fide" guest in the home of a hospitable friend.

∎ You can't have liquor in your club or your hotel, unless you have a legal residence there.

∎ You can't buy fruit juice after it starts to ferment.

No Ceremony is Held

Women Get the Vote

August 27, 1920—At 8 o'clock this morning the 19th amendment to the U.S. Constitution was quietly signed into law by Secretary of State Bainbridge Colby. It was the "crowning glory" for the women of America who have been leading the bitter struggle for suffrage. At last the vote was theirs.

The signing was held without ceremony at Colby's home. Many of those who had fought for women's suffrage were disappointed by the lack of fanfare. Noticeably absent were any members of the National Women's Party or the National Suffrage Association, led by Carrie Chapman Catt.

None of the suffragists had been invited to witness the historic event. And there were no photographers or cameramen present to record the moment, as suffragists had hoped.

Colby said of the private signing, "It was decided not to accompany this simple ministerial action on my part with any ceremony or setting. . . . I have contented myself with the performance in the simplest manner (prescribed) by law."

Colby defended his decision to keep the signing private. He compared it to the "simple fashion" with which Admiral Dewey went to war in the Philipines. ". . . How he came up on deck, wiping the egg stains of breakfast from the ends of his moustache, how he observed the disposition of the enemy ships and that of his own vessels . . . how he turned quietly, removing a well-smoked cigar from his lips, and said simply, 'You may fire when ready.' That is much the way I felt about this. And I say to the women of America, 'You may fire when ready.'"

The Secretary was asked what was to become of the pen he used to sign the suffrage proclamation. "I wouldn't be surprised, if it found its way to the Smithsonian Institution as part of an exhibit," Colby answered.

Meanwhile, President Woodrow Wilson sent greetings to the suffrage workers who were meeting in Washington, D.C.

Harding Expresses Support

The largest celebration was held in Marion, Ohio, on the front porch of Senator Warren G. Harding's home. The senator is the Republican candidate for president.

Senator Harding expressed his pleasure at the success of the suffrage cause. "I rejoice with you in the conferring of suffrage to the women citizenship of this nation," he said to the crowd of women gathered in his yard.

Senator Harding also had another message for women. He urged women voters to refrain from forming a third political party. "We have always had two great parties. And great parties are the only means we have for the effective expression of popular sentiment." ∎

The women's suffrage movement fought a long struggle to obtain a woman's right to vote. Their efforts were rewarded when the 19th Amendment to the Constitution became law.

Mexican Revolutionary
Villa Raids American Towns

Pancho Villa (center) and some of his followers.

How could an illiterate peasant get the best of one of America's great military leaders? It couldn't have happened. But it did.

Two months before the United States entered the Great War in Europe, it was retreating in defeat from Mexico. America's soldiers had simply been outmaneuvered by the Mexican revolutionary, Pancho Villa.

Born Doroteo Arango in 1878, Francisco "Pancho" Villa had been fighting for control of the Mexican government since the Revolution of 1910. Venustiano Carranza, another revolutionary, had come to power in 1914. But he was unacceptable to Villa and also to Emiliano Zapata. Villa and his men controlled northern Mexico; Zapata roamed the south. Between them they hoped to weaken Carranza's forces through heavy, hit-and-run fighting in the countryside.

Of the two revolutionary camps, America had been most wary of Villa and his army of *"villistas."* Villa and his men had no qualms about raiding American towns in southern Arizona and New Mexico. Their purpose was to "harrass" the "capitalistic" mining interests located there—particularly the Phelps-Dodge Mining Company of Bisbee, Arizona.

The worst outrage happened in January 1916. Villa and his men raided a train bound from Chihuahua City, Mexico, for a New Mexico mining town. They rounded up 16 American passengers on board, robbed them, then shot them all, except for one man who hid in the train's toilet. Villa claimed the action was taken because President Woodrow Wilson had recently given diplomatic recognition to the Carranza government.

President Wilson's response to the murders was immediate. He sent American soldiers to northern Mexico under the leadership of General John J. Pershing. It was called the "Pershing Punitive Expedition." But a year after Pershing and his soldiers went into Mexico, they came out empty-handed. The Americans had not been able to "disperse" the foxy Villa and his *villistas* as they had hoped they could.

Despite the dangers posed by the *villistas*, the drama was hard to resist. Residents of American towns near Villa's northern Mexico battle-grounds were fascinated by the Mexican bandit's raids. It was reported that the townspeople of Bisbee climbed the surrounding hills to get a better view of the fighting going on below. Numerous spectators have taken photographs which are now proudly exhibited in family albums. ∎

The Mexican bandit Villa and his men raided many towns in southern Arizona and New Mexico.

Ford Introduces the First Assembly Line

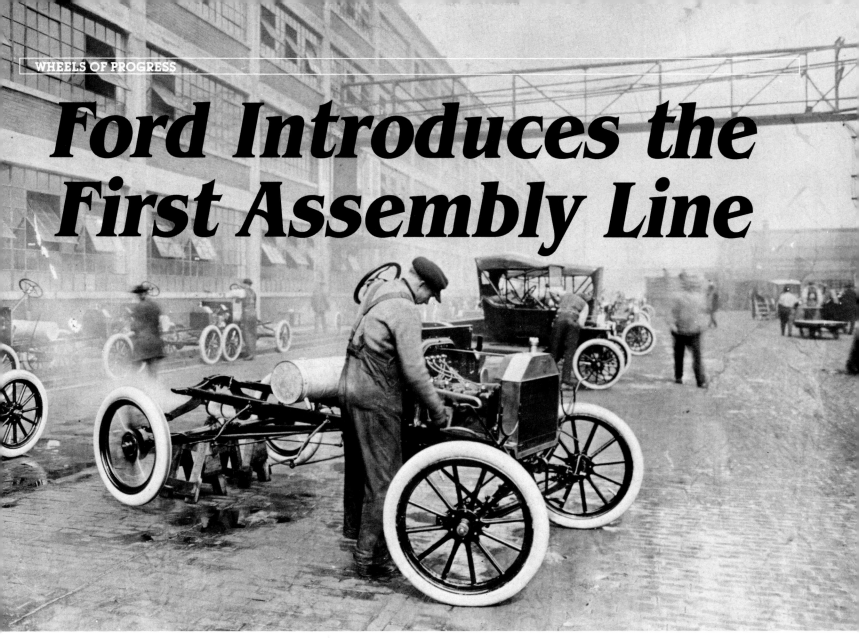

Henry Ford was only one of many automobile producers, but he was by far the most successful and innovative. Above, workmen in his Michigan plant mount an engine to the frame of a Model T.

The debut of the Model T Ford in 1908 was the marvel of the decade. Not only did it mark the beginning of Henry Ford's automobile empire, but it had a major impact on the entire young industry.

Five years later, on October 7, 1913, Ford made news again. This time he revolutionized the production of his own cars by unveiling the world's first assembly line. This event turned all production industries upside down. No one had ever seen anything as efficient and timesaving as the "line" Ford installed at his Highland Park, Michigan, plant.

Before the assembly line, workers had to walk to each car to put pieces of it in place. This was a slow, time-wasting process. Now cars were being carried *to* the workmen on a 250-foot-long assembly line. With the aid of the moving line, a whole car could be put together in less than three hours. ⇨

The immediate impact of Ford's assembly line was increased production. Within a year, Ford had produced 250,000 new cars. This was good news to Americans waiting to buy the up-to-now scarce "horseless carriages."

Company Profits Soar

Even better, Ford was able to achieve a decade-long goal. With the assembly line producing so many more cars, he could offer the public a lower-priced model. In 1915, a Ford automobile could be purchased for $500—about half the price of his top-of-the-line model.

So successful was Ford with his assembly line that his company's profits soared to $60 million within a year. In response, Ford made another revolutionary move. He passed part of his profits on to his employees by voluntarily increasing wages. On January 15, 1915, Ford announced that he would institute a $5 minimum day wage. This amount of money was unheard of. In some cases it was nearly three times more than other factory workers made. Ford said that the added money would flow back into the economy. And that would mean more customers for the automobile makers, including Ford's competition, Chevrolet and Dodge.

In 1916, Ford announced that he was going to lower the price of his cars even further—to $250. His goal now was to get automobiles into rural areas. There, it was estimated, another million customers were ready to buy his cars.

By 1919, the great numbers of cars being sold were changing the nation itself. One government official said the health of the nation's economy depended on the development of roads and highways. ■

. . . a whole car could be put together in less than three hours.

Below, workmen inside the factory put finishing touches on the cars.

Ford's pride was the Model T like the one pictured above. Built in 1915, it was the first two-door sedan. Price: $975.

Ford's Competition: Chevrolet

Louis Chevrolet at Indianapolis Raceway

In winter of 1911, a Swiss-born race car driver named Louis Chevrolet announced the formation of the Chevrolet Motor Company of Michigan. The product, he said, would be a new, high-priced luxury car called the Chevrolet. The distinctive feature of the car was an engine that Chevrolet himself had perfected.

A trained mechanic, the 33-year-old Chevrolet was best known for breaking a speed record in 1905.

The event was New York's Morris Park automobile race. Driving a Fiat, Chevrolet won by traveling 68 mph.

In May 1920, Chevrolet's younger brother, Gaston, made the news. He won the Indianapolis 500 speed race, then in its ninth year. But in November of that year, Gaston, 28, was killed. He met his end in a fiery crash during a Los Angeles race for the title of "Speed King of the Year."

The Panama Canal under construction, January 1913

Wilson Blasts Final Barrier to Panama Canal

October 10, 1913—With the simple press of a button, President Woodrow Wilson today changed the course of world travel. At 2:02 P.M. from his White House office, the President sent a spark of electricity 4,000 miles across telegraph cable to Panama. There it touched off 1,600 pounds of dynamite. A moment later, a great cheer went up from the 3,000 spectators on the scene.

The blast blew up the better part of the Gamboa Dike. The dike was the last physical barrier to the long-awaited passage between the Atlantic and Pacific oceans, the Panama Canal.

As the explosion occurred, a shower of water, mud, and rock shot high in the air. "It spread out as it went upward, the whole (area) heavily veiled in a cloud of smoke," one observer said.

As spectacular and successful as the explosion was, it did not completely open the canal. One spot in the waterway is still blocked by a huge mass of earth and rock called the Cucaracha Slide. And not all of Gamboa Dike was destroyed. "Utter demolition was not carried out," officials reported. Sources said officials feared that the shock would damage the railroad trestle crossing the cut.

Complete clearance of the canal for steamship and cargo travel is not expected until June of next year. But today's blast did open the canal to navigation by small craft. The first boat in the water was a canoe manned by two Americans. ■

How the Canal Brings the Whole World Closer

How much difference will the Canal make? The chart below shows just how much. Notice the length of the old water routes around the southern tip of South America. Then compare that with the new route through the Panama Canal in Central America:

	Old Route	New Route
■ Distance from Atlantic to Pacific side of Panama	10,719 miles	41 miles
■ New York to San Francisco	13,400 miles	5,300 miles
■ New York to Hawaiian Islands	12,800 miles	7,000 miles
■ Liverpool, England to San Francisco	13,731 miles	8,038 miles

A Canal Hero Misses the Ceremony

Millions of gallons of water flowed through the blasted Gamboa Dike in Panama today. But one man was not on hand for the cheering. Lieutenant Colonel D. D. Gaillard, one of the canal's most talented engineers, lay ill in a Baltimore, Maryland hospital. Doctors say he is suffering from a brain disease. They blame his illness on the tropical climate of Panama, where he has worked for the past nine years.

The New Waterway: Facts and Figures

- **Length:** 42½ miles
- **Cost:** $375 million
- **Dirt Excavated:** 242 million cubic yards
- **Time Necessary for Passage:** 10 to 12 hours
- **Earlier Attempts:** Spain conceived the idea in 1814. In 1824, the United States government made the first survey, but did not act.
- **History of Completion:** Actual construction of the canal began in 1882 by a French company headed by the man who built the Suez Canal; the company failed. In 1904, the United States took over canal construction after signing a treaty with Panama. Construction began May 4, 1904.

The World's Greatest Athlete

Jim Thorpe competing in the broad jump at the 1912 Olympics.

The story of Jim Thorpe's athletic career is one of great triumph and bitter disappointment.

In 1912, Thorpe stunned the sports world at the Summer Olympics in Stockholm, Sweden. He became the first athlete ever to win gold medals in both the pentathlon and the decathlon. Those two events are considered the greatest test of an athlete's all-around strength, agility, and speed. Thorpe's decathlon score was so high that it set a world record.

At the Games' closing ceremonies, the King of Sweden presented Thorpe with his medals. "You sir, are the greatest athlete in the world," the King told him. The shy, young American Indian could only reply, "Thanks, King."

Thorpe returned to the United States as a national hero. A big parade through the streets of New York City was held in his honor. He was famous throughout the country. It was an accomplishment, that while growing up, Thorpe could hardly have imagined.

Jim Thorpe was born in Indian Territory (now the state of Oklahoma) in 1886. He and his family were part of the Sac-Fox tribe. His Indian name was "Bright Path."

Jim Thorpe grew up in two worlds. In the Sac-Fox world he learned how to hunt, fish, run, and wrestle. But he also received a formal American education. And it was while attending the Carlisle Indian school in Pennsylvania that Thorpe was introduced to competitive sports.

In 1911, while at Carlisle, Thorpe was named an all-American halfback in football. In one game he kicked a football 83 yards, nearly the full length of the field. His coach at Carlisle was "Pop" Warner. It was Warner who turned Thorpe into an all-around athlete good enough to join the 1912 U.S. Olympic team.

Medals Taken Away

After his Olympic triumph, Jim Thorpe's future athletic career seemed unlimited. But about a month after the Games, Thorpe was stripped of his medals by the Olympic Committee.

The committee had ruled that Thorpe was not an amateur. Reports had come to them that Thorpe had played professional baseball in the years before the Olympics. As a pitcher on a North Carolina baseball team called the Rocky Mount, he had earned $15 a week.

Although the money he earned wasn't much, it did mean that Thorpe was a professional athlete. As such he was ineligible to compete in the Olympics. Only athletes of amateur standing are allowed in the Games.

Thorpe was bitterly disappointed at the committee's actions. He claimed he didn't know there was anything wrong with playing pro ball. "I was not very wise to the ways of the world," he told the press.

Still, the committee did not change its decision. Thorpe was asked to turn over his medals to the men who had finished second in the two events. One of the men didn't want Thorpe's medal. He said it belonged to the man who had won it, no matter what the committee said.

As disappointed as he was, losing his medals didn't stop Thorpe from competing in sports. During the decade he played major league baseball for the New York Giants, Cincinnati Reds, and the Boston Braves. He also became a professional football player, and he has been named the first president of the American Professional Football Association.

To his many fans, Thorpe remains the "world's greatest athlete." ∎

Athletics, Red Sox Tops in Baseball

Two Great Teams

Two teams from the young American League dominated major league baseball for the past ten years. The Boston Red Sox won four World Championships this decade, and the Philadelphia Athletics won three. The American League has only been in existence since 1901. So it was a great showing by the newer baseball clubs.

The Athletics were the team to beat during the early years of the decade. Much of their success was due to their part-owner and manager, Cornelius McGillicuddy. Known to baseball fans everywhere as Connie Mack, he's famous for his oddly formal style of dress in the dugout. Mack guided his team to four pennants and three World Series victories between 1910 and 1914.

Fans everywhere admired the A's famous "$100,000 infield." The outstanding players were: first baseman Stuffy McInnis, second baseman Eddie Collins, shortstop Jack Barry, and third baseman Frank "Home Run" Baker. With that top-notch infield, the A's led the league in hitting and fielding from 1910 to 1914.

The Boston Red Sox were the other powerhouse team. The boys from Boston won the pennant in 1912, 1915, 1916, and 1918. And each time, they went on to defeat their National League opponents to capture the World Series.

The Red Sox team featured a strong pitching staff led by a young left-hander named Babe Ruth. Ruth joined the Sox in 1914. He won 65 games for them in the next three seasons. But it was in World Series play that the young southpaw really showed his stuff.

In the 1916 Series, Ruth pitched and won the longest World Series game to date. It was a 14-inning 2–1 decision over the Brooklyn Robins. Then in the 1918 Series, Ruth won two more games, beating the Chicago Cubs. During these two Series, he set a record by pitching 29 straight scoreless innings. In addition, the talented Ruth showed great promise as a hitter. During the 1918 season he hit 11 home runs to lead the League.

Baseball's popularity took a back seat during the war years. In 1918, the government ruled that baseball was a "nonessential" occupation. Many players were drafted to fight. Others went to work in war production factories. That year the season was shortened to 125 games, and the World Series was played in early September.

When the war ended, public attention quickly returned to the game. After a successful 1919 season, the Cincinnati Reds defeated the Chicago White Sox in a closely fought World Series. At the time, no fan could have suspected that the Series would cause a baseball crisis a year later. The 1919 World Series would be the focus of the biggest scandal in sports history: the "Black Sox" betting scandal (see following story). ∎

Below, members of the 1914 Philadelphia A's at spring training in Jacksonville, Florida. The A's went to camp that year as baseball's defending World Champions.

Philadelphia A's manager Connie Mack

White Sox Admit Throwing Series

Betting Scandal Rocks Baseball

September 28, 1920—The baseball world was rocked by scandal today. Eight members of the Chicago White Sox admitted to "throwing" last year's World Series to the Cincinnati Reds in return for $100,000. The Reds won the Series 5 games to 3.

The accused Chicago players are said to have intentionally played to lose the first, second, and final games of the 1919 Series. They are now being referred to as the "Black Sox."

Sox pitcher Eddie Cicotte admitted before a grand jury hearing in Chicago that he received $10,000 for his part in the scheme. The money came from the agent of a gambling syndicate.

A total of $100,000 was reportedly passed to the eight players by the syndicate. The gamblers then won large amounts of money when they made bets on the "known" outcome of the Series. Not all the money has been accounted for, and the investigation is continuing.

Popular Sox outfielder "Shoeless" Joe Jackson confessed that he was paid $5,000 for his part in throwing the games.

Also involved in the "Black Sox Scandal" were pitcher "Lefty" Williams who reportedly received $10,000; third baseman "Buck" Weaver, $5,000; outfielder "Happy" Felsch, $1,000; shortstop "Swede" Risberg, $2,000; first baseman "Chick" Gandil, $20,000; and utility infielder Fred McMullin, $15,000.

As the news of the scandal was released to the public, the manager of the White Sox suspended the eight players. He said "we would rather take chances for the pennant with an honest bunch of scrubs than with a crowd of stars under suspicion."

Famous Pitcher Tells the Story

Cicotte was the first to tell his story before the grand jury. At one point the pitcher broke down in tears. He called the episode a disgrace to his family. He said he cursed the day he "got mixed up in this thing."

"I have lived a thousand years in the last year," he said. "My poor kids—why did I do it?"

"Never mind why, now, Eddie," an attorney said. "Just tell the jury what was done."

Cicotte told the jury of the discussions that were held between the players and the syndicate's "go-between." He said they talked about how much money the players would get, and when and how they would get it.

"The night before the first game," Cicotte said between sobs, "I found the money. Someone had placed $10,000 under my pillow."

Cicotte lost two games during the Series, and Lefty Williams lost three. Despite their agreement to "throw" the games, Jackson and Weaver actually played very well. Jackson hit .375 and Weaver hit .324 in the Series. ■

"It Ain't True, Is It Joe?"

Several hundred youngsters ranging in age from 6 to 16 stood outside the Criminal Courts building in Chicago yesterday. They were waiting to catch a glimpse of their former idol, "Shoeless" Joe Jackson.

One young man stepped up to the outfielder and grabbed at his coat sleeve. "It ain't true, is it Joe?" the boy asked.

"Yes, kid, I'm afraid it is," Jackson replied.

The boys opened a path for the ballplayer and stood in silence until he passed from sight.

"Well, I never would have thought it," the lad said sadly to a reporter.

White Sox outfielder "Shoeless" Joe Jackson was one of eight players involved in baseball's betting scandal.

America's "Yankee Doodle Dandy"

George M. Cohan is a man of many talents. Composer, playwright, and performer, Cohan has become one of the brightest lights on Broadway.

Cohan was born into a vaudeville family in 1878. By the age of 15 he was performing on stage as a "song and dance" man with his parents and his sister. He was 23 when his first play was produced on Broadway. The play starred him and his family, billed as the "Four Cohans." Between 1904 and 1920, Cohan and his partner, Sam H. Harris, produced numerous plays, all of them successful.

Two of Cohan's popular plays of the last decade were *Get Rich Quick* and *Little Johnny Jones*.

Cohan has gained fame as a songwriter as well. Among his most popular songs are, "Give My Regards to Broadway," "You're a Grand Old Flag," and the patriotic "Over There." Cohan composed the latter song on the day America entered the Great War. It served as a great morale booster for American troops fighting in Europe.

That song helped earn Cohan his famous nickname, "Yankee Doodle Dandy." He claims to have been born on July 4. ∎

(Right) American showman George M. Cohan as he appeared in the hit play, *Little Johnny Jones*. (Top) George M. Cohan and his performing family. Left to right: father, Jerry; mother, Helen; and sister, Josephine.

The Birth of the Motion Picture

By 1915, filmmakers had been making motion pictures for more than a decade. But it wasn't until then that the public saw its first full-length production. That movie, *The Birth of a Nation* was directed by D. W. Griffith.

The three-hour epic opened on March 3 to a mix of praise and criticism. *The Birth of a Nation* told the story of a white southern family surviving the Civil War. Many people felt that the film was racist. One of the heroes of the movie was a member of the Ku Klux Klan. The Negro characters were portrayed as either threatening or foolish. Protests and boycotts greeted the film in many cities where it opened.

Even with this content, the film itself was praised for its "sweep and grandeur." Critics said it raised the motion picture to the "status of art."

But it was more than art. It turned out to be a windfall of profits, too. *The Birth of a Nation* was a big hit with audiences. In spite of its controversial storyline, it was the first movie to be distributed to independent theaters across the country. Before that, motion pictures were shown in only a few cities. *The Birth of a Nation* has changed all that. Now, as long as a town has a theater of any kind, movies are available to everyone. ∎

Motion picture director D. W. Griffith

A scene from the movie, *The Birth of a Nation*. The Civil War epic was both praised and criticized by people around the country.

Mary Pickford

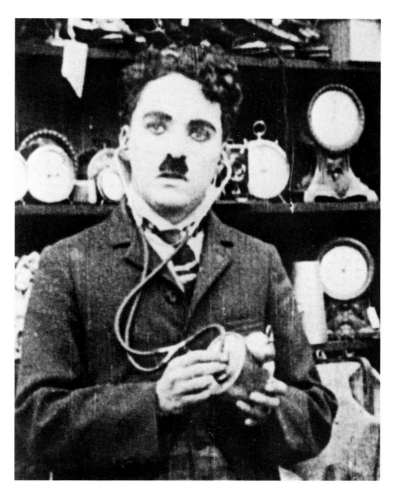

Charlie Chaplin

America's Sweetheart and the "Little Tramp"

With her curls and innocent-looking face, Mary Pickford has become everybody's favorite motion picture star. Nicknamed "America's Sweetheart," Pickford has starred in such films as the 1914 hit, *Tess of the Storm Country*.

Pickford was one of the first actresses to receive public attention. Many other performers have remained almost unknown. Directors and producers didn't think the actors were nearly as important as the movie itself. That attitude changed when independent producer Carl Laemmle lured Pickford away from her studio, Biograph. He did this by offering her two reasons for leaving: star billing and a lot of money.

By the end of 1915, Mary Pickford was one of the richest of the "new" movie stars. Her old salary had been $175 a week. Now she was taking home $10,000 a week. And that was only the beginning. By 1919, Pickford was making so much money that she and three other movie artists formed their own movie studio. They called it United Artists.

Pickford's partners in United Artists included her husband, the romantic actor, Douglas Fairbanks. The other two were director D. W. Griffith, and a British-born comedian named Charlie Chaplin.

Chaplin had come to America in 1913. He became noted for starring in the zany comedies produced by Mack Sennett. Sennett's movies were high-speed comedies, heavy with chase scenes. Moviegoers loved them. But critics complained that they were nothing more than "custard pie comedy."

Chaplin agreed. He believed that comedy should be subtle. And he also felt that the characters should be well developed. As early as 1913 Chaplin was working on the character that made him a star. It was "Charlie the little tramp," a sad, silly, sympathetic character first seen in the 1915 hit, *The Tramp*.

The Tramp became a huge hit with the public. In the next two years he starred in several more hits. And by the end of 1917, Chaplin was making an astounding $1 million a year. ∎

Woodrow Wilson
A Man of Peace

Woodrow
Wilson

Thomas Woodrow Wilson was born in 1856 in Staunton, Virginia. The son of a Presbyterian minister, Wilson grew up in a family that strongly believed in both religion and education. This background led him first to a career as a lawyer, and then as a college professor.

Wilson became president of Princeton University in 1902. He was the first nonclergyman ever to be appointed to the position. It was as an educator that Wilson first gained national attention. During his time at Princeton, he was responsible for many popular reforms. One of his ideas was to put less emphasis on the lecture hall as the main method of instruction. Instead, Wilson favored "individual instruction" in a classroom setting. That system has now been copied by universities around the country.

Wilson's political career began in 1910. That year he was drafted by the Democratic party to run for the governorship of New Jersey. He won the election by a huge margin.

As governor, Wilson again gained national notice. He pushed many reforms in the areas of education, employment, and consumer protection through the state legislature. Experts praised Wilson's reforms; they said he had changed the face of New Jersey's government. Democratic party leaders took notice as well.

Wilson's rise within the Democratic party was a fast one. Within two years he was the key spokesman for the party's liberal wing. By 1911 he was clearly a candidate for his party's presidential nomination. After a tough and lengthy convention fight, Wilson was nominated on the 46th ballot. He then defeated both William Howard Taft and Teddy Roosevelt in the election of 1912.

In 1914, Wilson was responsible for the passage of the Clayton Anti-Trust Act. The bill legalized labor unions, peaceful picketing, boycotts, and strikes. It was this bill that labor leaders celebrated as labor's "new bill of rights." But many in government and business considered the bill too "liberal."

"Fourteen Points" Basis for Peace

Wilson ran for reelection in 1916. He stressed America's neutral position in the European war. His campaign slogan was: He's the man "who kept us out of war." A year later it was a claim he couldn't make. Reacting to German submarine warfare, Wilson asked Congress to declare war on the Central Powers in April 1917. (See page 20.) When the war ended in 1918, Wilson left for Europe and the signing of the peace treaty at Versailles.

The basis of the peace treaty was Wilson's famous "Fourteen Points" which he put forth in 1918. Among the points was his idea for an international body called the League of Nations. Wilson's League would be dedicated to peacefully settling disputes among nations. His idea was made part of the peace agreement signed in Paris.

Wilson's ideas for peace earned him respect and praise throughout Europe. But his ideas were not well received at home. Many in Congress have opposed him. The Senate has voted against America's entering any organization with the European powers.

In September 1919, Wilson toured the United States making speeches. He attempted to raise popular support for his League. In 20 days Wilson traveled some 8,200 miles by train. He delivered 40 speeches in 14 Midwestern and Western states. On the night of September 25, Wilson collapsed in Colorado from "nervous exhaustion."

"I guess I'm all in," the president said after the collapse. At the time, a spokesman said the president's illness was not serious. Later, it was revealed that he had suffered a stroke. The stroke has left Wilson partially paralyzed. ∎

Vladimir Lenin
Revolutionary

The man now known to the world as Lenin was born Vladimir Ilyich Ulyanov in 1870. The son of a school administrator, Lenin grew up in Simbirsk, a small town alongside the Volga River. From boyhood, revolutionary ideas were close at hand.

His older brother, Alexander, was a university student who joined a revolutionary terrorist group called "the People's Will." The group came to attention in 1887 when the tsar's police uncovered a plot to assassinate Alexander III, Tsar Nicholas's father.

Alexander Ulyanov was among the members arrested after the plot was discovered. He was hanged two days later at age 19, despite pleas from the Ulyanov family. In court, Alexander passionately claimed that he was not a traitor to his country. "I have had one aim," he said. "And that is to serve the unfortunate Russian people."

Because of his brother's activities, Lenin was watched closely during his own university years. Before long, he began serious revolutionary study and writing on his own. When this activity was discovered, he was expelled from the University of Kazan in southern Russia. But that did not stop him. He studied law by correspondence from the University of St. Petersburg. He graduated at the top of his class in 1891.

Vladimir Lenin

Lenin is a political follower of Karl Marx, the German-born father of communism. During his early twenties he became dedicated to Marx's "proletarian revolution," or people's revolt. Soon he began to rewrite some of Marx's ideas to fit conditions in tsarist Russia. Lenin's work soon gained fame and favor among Russia's educated citizens and European socialists. As his fame grew, he wrote bolder, more revolutionary works. Those writings raised the suspicions of the tsar's government even more.

In the late 1890s, Lenin was exiled and imprisoned in Siberia.

Later he was deported to Europe as a "seditious" influence. It was in 1901 that he began using the pseudonym Lenin. The name was first used in stories he wrote in the revolutionary newspaper, *Iskra* ("Spark").

In 1903 Lenin became leader of the Bolshevik party. For the next 14 years he continued his revolutionary work both inside and outside of Russia. That work climaxed in the revolution of 1917 which brought him to power. ■

Champion of the Common Man
Louis D. Brandeis

Louis D. Brandeis

From his earliest days as an attorney in Boston, Louis D. Brandeis has fought for the "common man's" interests. He spent many years in private practice working for consumers, labor unions, and small stockholders in large corporations. Frequently this work was unpaid.

A liberal thinker, Brandeis has become known as the "people's attorney." He worked with strikers in New York. He defended workers in Oregon who wanted a 10-hour workday and better wages for women. He has been a leader in the Zionist movement which seeks a homeland for the world's displaced Jews. And in 1914 he wrote the sensational book *Other People's Money and How the Bankers Use It.* Experts called the book a "brilliant analysis" of how the rich influence the life of the average American.

In 1913, President Woodrow Wilson asked Brandeis to join his cabinet, but Brandeis refused. Three years later, Wilson nominated him to a seat on the Supreme Court.

Brandeis's appointment angered many people. His record was too liberal for many in Congress. He had too often sided against government and big money interests in his campaigns for the "average American." And his Jewish faith was used against him. There were those in Congress who refused to put the first Jew on the Supreme Court.

In the end, though, Brandeis was confirmed by Congress. As many expected, he has written opinions that protect the rights of the common people. But some still complain that he is a thorn in the side of Big Business. ∎

The Socialist Candidate
Eugene Debs

Eugene Debs

May 9, 1920—For the fifth time since 1900, labor leader Eugene Victor Debs is running for president of the United States.

This time around, however, Debs did not receive his nomination in person. At the time he was nominated, Debs was sitting in a federal prison cell. He was being held on charges of espionage. The indictment was brought against him in 1918 during a roundup of suspected Communists. The charge has been criticized by socialists and nonsocialists alike.

Debs's nomination was forwarded by some 6,000 members of the Socialist party, the party Debs founded. The members held their convention at Madison Square Garden in New York City. A socialist spokesman predicts that Debs will win two to three million votes in this November's election.

Debs is a railroad man-turned-labor leader. In 1893 he founded the American Railway Union. In 1894, he was imprisoned on charges stemming from that year's Pullman railroad strike. While in prison, Debs studied the works of socialist philosophers and economists.

In 1897 he turned his railway union into the Social Democratic Party of America. It was later renamed the Socialist Party of America.

Debs first ran for president in 1900, then again in 1904, 1908, and 1912. In 1912, he received nearly 900,000 votes. ∎

Fighting for Women's Rights

Margaret Sanger

Women doing women's work rarely make the news. But public health nurse Margaret Higgins Sanger continues to shock the country. She believes that women have the right to decide how many children to have. Her campaign is for family planning by using contraceptives.

Sanger was born in Corning, New York, in 1883, the sixth of 11 children. After teaching briefly, she practiced nursing on New York City's Lower East Side. Because of her experience there, she has come to believe that poverty is one result of overly-large families. She also believes that too many women die from illegal abortions. What's needed, says

Sanger, is a national program of birth control.

Sanger's program and her outspokenness are illegal. The Comstock Law of 1873 prohibits distribution of information on contraception. But the law hasn't stopped the determined Sanger from speaking out and publishing numerous articles. Two of her best known articles are, *What Every Mother Should Know* and *What Every Girl Should Know*.

In 1914, Sanger founded the National Birth Control League. In the same year she established a monthly magazine called *The Woman Rebel*.

The following year she was arrested for sending birth control

information through the mails. The pamphlet was titled *Family Limitation*. It was printed in English, Italian, and Yiddish. The criminal charges against her were later dropped.

In 1916, Sanger opened the first birth control clinic in America. It was located in Brooklyn, New York. She was quickly arrested and sentenced to 30 days in prison for this offense.

But Sanger's arrests haven't stopped her. She refuses to give up the fight. Sanger is presently traveling across the country giving speeches and lectures. Her hope is to persuade both the public and the medical profession of the importance of her cause. ■

Margaret Sanger

DELCO-LIGHT
Increases Farm Efficiency

1—Saves Time and Labor
2—Attracts Labor to the Farm
3—Keeps Boys and Girls on the Farm
4—Solves the Retired Farmer Problem
5—Lightens the Burdens of Farm Women

Encourages Sociability—Makes the Farm Home
the Finest Place in the World

No. 3

Keeps the Young Folks On the Farm

Delco-Light brings to the farm all the modern conveniences that formerly attracted the boys and girls to the city.

It provides an abundance of bright, clean, economical electric light for house, grounds and outbuildings.

It pumps water and makes possible the convenience of running water and a modern bath.

It furnishes power to do electrically many of the household tasks that heretofore have made farm life burdensome.

In a word—Delco-Light improves living conditions—makes the farm home more cheerful and attractive—and at the same time increases farm efficiency and actually pays for itself in time and labor saved.

Self-Cranking	*Ball Bearings*
Air Cooled	*Thick Plate Long-*
No Belts	*Lived Battery*
One Place to Oil	*Uses Kerosene*

Prices $395 to $465 *Except in the Far West and Canada*

The Domestic Engineering Company, Dayton, Ohio

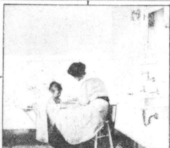

OVER 50,000 DELCO-LIGHT PLANTS IN ACTUAL USE